THE BOOK OF THE LOVER
AND THE BELOVED

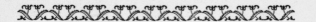

THE BOOK OF THE LOVER
AND THE BELOVED

TRANSLATED FROM THE CATALAN
OF RAMÓN LULL WITH AN INTRO-
DUCTORY ESSAY BY

E. ALLISON PEERS

LONDON
SOCIETY FOR PROMOTING
CHRISTIAN KNOWLEDGE
NEW YORK AND TORONTO: THE MACMILLAN COMPANY
1923

248.13
L969

74462

PREFACE

MORE than six centuries have passed since this
little Majorcan classic was written, and, so far
as I can find, it has never once been translated into
English. Such an omission can only be explained
by our comparative ignorance of the treasures of
Spanish Mysticism, and perhaps in part by the fact
that Lull wrote, not in Castilian, but in a little-
known though beautiful idiom, that of Catalonia.

It would have been attractive to reproduce the
original version of the book together with this translation, and even more so to have translated the
whole of *Blanquerna*, of which it forms a part. I
hope that both these projects may be realised in the
future, together with the translations of (at least) *Els
Cent Noms de Deu, El Desconort*, and some of the
short hymns and poems. But it seemed best to
begin by making known some of Lull's best work to
as wide a circle of readers as possible. Accordingly,
while following, as a rule, the oldest text (which is of
the fourteenth century) I have not scrupled to add
to my translation a few passages found only in the
editions of Paris (1505) and Valencia (1521), which
illuminate the author's thought, or seem in other
ways to be of real value.

On the other hand, I have not allowed myself,
through a desire to expound Lull's ideas, to sub-
stitute paraphrase for faithful and exact translation.
Very few liberties have been taken with the text, and

these only where a slight expansion or change of construction has served to bring out the meaning of an otherwise quite obscure word or phrase.   Essentially, therefore, the reader has Lull's own vivid and forceful words, with the impediment of a foreign language removed.

E. ALLISON PEERS

The University, Liverpool.
    Jan. 19, 1923.

INTRODUCTORY ESSAY

THE average man has seldom understood the Mystic. He conceives the Mystic Life, with its ceaseless spiritual activity, and its restlessness which knows no stay till it reaches its goal, as a life of tranquillity, if not of indolence and ease. He has no conception of what it really is, and for that, perhaps, he should not be blamed. But not content with misinterpreting the mystic's life, he presently becomes more daring; he asserts that mysticism is essentially ' unpractical,' and that one whose aim is to reach the state of Union with God must necessarily be as a fool in his relations with the world. Here the average man is grossly, inexcusably mistaken. His error has again and again been exposed, confuted, disproved by example after example to the contrary. Yet, for all that, it seems to thrive in the average mind.

Now, if the story of one man's career could suffice to destroy the mistaken idea that the mystic is an unpractical dreamer, that man would surely be the Majorcan Ramón Lull, the ' Apostle of Africa.' Lull lived far back in the thirteenth century, not long after the days of St. Francis of Assisi, whose disciple he was. He gives us, as it were, a prevision of the splendours of that Golden Age of Mysticism which dawned for Spain three hundred years after his birth. His mystic writings—and especially his BOOK OF THE LOVER AND THE

BELOVED—are full of the purest and noblest spirituality, compounded with the quintessence of love. ' If ye will have fire,' he cries, ' O ye that love, come light your lanterns at my heart.' His famous phrase, ' He who loves not lives not,' sums up his inspiration. Yet Lull was no cloistered visionary. His life is full of romance and adventure : so crowded with incident is it that many pages will not suffice even to summarise its principal happenings. His capacities showed the rare combination of scholar and man of affairs : he was both these, and he was also the man of God. To the service of his Master, for Whom alone he lived, and for Whom he died, Lull was able to bring the full and complete tribute of an efficient and active body, a superb mind, and an ardent, unconquerable spirit.

I

RAMÓN LULL was born in Palma, the capital of Majorca, on January 25, 1235. His father had taken part in the conquest of Majorca from the Saracens some six years earlier, and for his services had received the gift of an estate, which his son inherited. The boy was brought up as a page in the royal court of Majorca, and, in spite of a sound religious education and the interest and favour of the King, he had hardly reached years of discretion when he began to lead a careless and dissolute life. His biographers tell of how the King, to ſtop his degrading practices, married him to a certain Dª. Blanca Picañy, but without thereby reforming him in the leaſt. Lull was chiefly enamoured of a Genoese lady, so passionately that he dared one day to ride on horseback into the Church of St. Eulalia, where she was engaged in devotion. Eventually she herself arreſted his intrigues. Receiving from him some gallant verses on the theme of her bosom, she called him into her presence, and, uncovering herself before him, disclosed a malignant cancer by which her breaſt was slowly being consumed.

This terrible shock marked the firſt ſtage in Lull's conversion. He went back to the palace another man—as taciturn and sombre as he had formerly been gay and jovial. The tradition may well be true that he saw at this time a vision of the Crucified, saying, ' Ramón, follow Me ' : he himself in some lines of autobiography tells us of five such visions, though when they occurred is not certain. Be this as it may, he turned from his evil life and fixed his affeċtions on God :

When I was grown and knew the world and its vanities, I began to do evil and entered on sin. Forgetting the true God I went after carnal things. But it pleased Jesus Christ in His great pity to present Himself to me five

3

times as if crucified, that I might remember Him and set my love on Him, doing what I could that He might be known through all the world and the truth be taught concerning the great Trinity and the Incarnation. And thus I was inspired and moved by so great love, that I loved no other thing but that He should be honoured, and I began to do Him willing service.[1]

From the first, as these lines significantly bear evidence, Lull's new ideals were directed towards specific objects. He was set upon the conversion of the Jews and Mohammedans who figured so largely in thirteenth-century Spain. And setting aside emotional methods as resolutely as the idea— so general then—of conversion by force, he began to ponder what he conceived to be worthy means of compassing his aim—a progressive and unanswerable appeal to the reason. A sermon heard on the Feast of St. Francis (October 4, 1266) supplied the spark which kindled Lull's plans into action. He sold all his land, with the exception of a portion retained for himself and his family, gave up his position of seneschal in the royal palace, and retired first to a Cistercian monastery and later to Mount Randa, near Palma, living there a life of study and meditation with the object of fitting himself to become a missionary to the Moslems.

The record of Lull's life in Mount Randa is one not only of prayer, fast and vigil, ecstasy and vision,

[1] *El Desconort*, ii.

4

but of the study of Arabic and the elaboration of his
scheme of a book which was to illuminate and convert the world. He believed this *Art General* to be
directly inspired by the Holy Spirit. Once it was
sufficiently developed he turned in his practical way
to means by which its study could be advanced. To
King James II of Majorca were explained the
scholar's vast plans for the conversion of Islam; the
King submitted them to one Bertram de Berengario,
a professor of theology, and, when satisfied of their
orthodoxy, endowed a college in Miramar for the
training in sciences and languages of thirteen
Franciscan missionaries to the Saracens (1275).
Thus one part of Lull's ideals was realised.

For a short time he remained at Miramar,
teaching Arabic and the *Art General*. But before
long we find him lecturing on the *Art* in Mor pellier,
which was part of the Majorcan kingdom Then
he is at Rome, where his enterprise is sancti ned by
the Pope, and a School of Oriental La guages
founded. He spends two years lecturing in the
University of Paris, learning all the time a vell as
teaching. A college is founded in Navarre rough
King Philip of France. Lull goes farther eld—
to Palestine, Egypt, Ethiopia and Moroc . In
1282 we read of his being back in France a in, at
Perpignan. Success continues to attend him, but
not in a measure that can satisfy his ardent soul.

Ever burning for more triumphs, he resolves at last to put the lukewarmness of Europe to shame, and to go himself to Africa as an Apostle of the Faith.

After some delay (the chronology of this period is very uncertain [1]) he set sail from Genoa, and landed in Tunis about 1291. Professing only a desire to learn the truth—to convert or be converted as events might prove—he began to debate in public with the Moslems, following his own logical method. He was only too successful. Many of the infidels, attracted by his reasoning, embraced Christianity ; but the monarch began to fear for his throne, and before long Lull found himself in prison. Condemned to death for his preaching, he was reprieved by the intercession of a Saracen of influence, and banished from Africa, leaving Tunis amid insults and blows, on pain of being stoned to death should he ever return. For a time he evaded his enemies and remained in the country, but a year of this life showed him its futility, and he returned to Naples. Here he remained writing and teaching for a time ; then he went to Rome (c. 1296), attempting unsuccessfully to obtain sanction for new missionary projects ; again we find him in Genoa, next in Paris (1297–8), back in Majorca, once more in Genoa (1300), then on a new campaign in Cyprus

[1] The date of *Blanquerna*, and hence of our classic, is put down at 1283.

and Armenia (1300–2), back *via* Rhodes and Malta, where he made stays, to Genoa and Paris (1303), Palma, Barcelona, Lyon and Montpellier (1305).[1] Here he saw both the King and Pope Clement V. With the former he planned a crusade for the Holy Land, but the latter, much occupied in other affairs, gave him no support.

Everywhere and always evangelisation filled his thoughts. No difficulty or objection, as the records of these years show, could curb his zeal; the thought of imprisonment or torture made no difference to his plans, while to die a martyr's death when his work should be done was his great ambition. 'Foolish Lover,' says an imaginary opponent to him in his little classic, 'why dost thou weary the body, throw away thy wealth and leave the joys of this world, and go about as an outcast of the people?' And his reply is the simplest imaginable. 'To honour my Beloved's Name, for He is hated and dishonoured by more men than honour and love Him.'

In 1306 Lull determined to make an attempt to preach once more in Africa. At the outset he was successful, founding a school at Bona, where he

---

[1] Lull is said to have been enticed to England (in the summer of 1305) by King Edward I, who believed him to have the secret of the Philosopher's Stone. But this story has no sure foundation.

7

first went. But on proceeding to Bugia, and beginning to preach in the market-place, he was promptly arrested, all but stoned by the crowds, summarily tried, and imprisoned in a loathsome dungeon with a view to later execution. Something in Lull's personality, however (or, as some say, the pleas of certain Catalan and Genoese inhabitants), saved him once more; he was even allowed the privilege of a disputation with a Mohammedan champion, and eventually was exiled again in the same year of his leaving Italy.

The ship in which he was returning suffered shipwreck off Pisa, where he landed and remained for two years. In Pisa he wrote a book incorporating his memorable dispute with the Saracen apologist and other experiences in Africa. But it would seem that these experiences had been modifying his belief in intellectual conversion, for he approached Pope Clement V again with proposals for a new crusade. Enthusiasm for crusades, however, was a thing of the past, and neither the Pope nor Italy as a whole gave the scheme any support.

So this dauntless fighter went once more to Paris, which at that time was in the grip of Averroism, and hence provided a new field for missionary effort. Seventy-three years old as he was, Lull lectured, wrote, and taught unceasingly against the infidel philosophy, and won for himself fresh glory, accomplishing in Europe what only physical force withheld from him in Africa. King Philip, his royal admirer, gave him the name of *docteur illuminé*, by which, in one or another of its translations, he is still known to-day.

The Council of Vienne (1311-2) gave Lull another of those opportunities which he was never slow to take. The picture of the venerable missionary at the feet of the Head of the Church, pouring forth his impassioned pleas for those enterprises which authority so hesitated to allow, is indeed a moving one. He painted the glory of recovering the Holy Places, the plight of the Christians in Armenia, and the peril which the Greeks were in from the Turks—themes not exhausted even after seven hundred years. These, however, were but a few of Lull's representations. The number of his requests which were granted was relatively small, but among them was a wider scheme than any yet sanctioned for a system of colleges for the teaching of missionary languages. This earnest of the continuance of his work must have encouraged beyond measure one who, in the natural course of life, was nearing the end of his activities.

Perhaps it was this, indeed, which inspired him to cross once more to Africa, to brave its terrors and to suffer martyrdom for the Faith at last—as from his conversion he had wished—if it might be the will of God. And the will of God it proved to be. On August 14, 1314, he set out from Palma for Bugia. On his arrival he began his work less openly than before, and for some months contrived to preach secretly, make conversions and confirm the faithful of earlier days. He passed to Tunis, where he had further success, but for some unknown reason was compelled to return to Bugia. Success made him bold. Feeling perhaps that the hour of supreme effort—even if it meant the supreme sacrifice—had come, he threw prudence to the winds, assembled a vast concourse, and, proclaiming himself that same Ramón who had formerly been condemned in Bugia, he preached once more the faith of the Saviour. This time the crowd broke loose, and not only clamoured for Lull's death, but took him out of the city and stoned him (June 30, 1315), even as a Jewish mob had stoned the first of Christian martyrs.

Various accounts are given of his burial. It seems that two Genoese merchants begged his body and carried it to Majorca, but some versions have it that a great pyramid of light aided them in their search for it, that life remained in the body until it reached Palma, and that adverse winds forced the vessel, which was making for Genoa, to land at Lull's birthplace. Here the body was received with the greatest sorrow and mourning, and buried with due solemnity in the sacristy of the convent of St. Francis of Assisi.

Ramón Lull was beatified by Pius IX. The title-page of his great romance, *Blanquerna*, calls him ' Doctor illuminate, Martyr unconquered of Jesus Christ, Master universal in all arts and sciences.' But in his own country Lull receives the simpler homage of a saint.

II

THE foregoing sketch, for all its brevity, will have emphasised more forcibly than much argument the practical and the scholarly sides of Lull's temperament. We shall say nothing here of the four hundred and eighty-six treatises [1] which he is known to have written, nor of the thousands of other works, no longer extant if indeed they ever existed, with which he is credited. Nor is there need to describe his system and doctrine, at once scholastic and popular in character. The *Libre de Amich e Amat*, which is here translated, is purely a mystical work, and this essay is concerned with the mystical side of

[1] Less than half of these works are theological. The remainder deal with the most diverse subjects, such as metaphysics, logic, ethics, physics, medicine, mathematics, and chemistry.

Lull's mind, so wonderfully illumined by the flame which burnt through his long life of self-sacrifice.

The Book of the Lover and the Beloved takes us from the African preachings and the disputations of the Sorbonne to those long night-watches and days of retreat which muſt always have accompanied them, but which we are apt to forget in contemplating that form of aĉtivity which the world counts greateſt. Or the thoughts which the *Book* gives us may firſt have come to the young convert in the solitude of his monaſtery and the retreat of Mount Randa. Rosselló, who some sixty years ago firſt published Lull's poems, interprets a passage from *Blanquerna* as autobiographical. It may well be so.

Being then in his hermitage he would rise at midnight, and, opening the windows of his cell, would fall to contemplating the heavens and the stars, and praying with all possible devotion, that his soul might be fixed upon God alone. . . . After long contemplation and much weeping, his custom was to enter the church and ring for mattins, and when his deacon appeared, to help him say them. At daybreak he celebrated Mass with devotion, and spoke of God with his deacon, that on God he might set his love. And as they talked together of God and His works, they both wept for the greatness of the devotion which their argument inspired in them. Then the deacon went into the garden and busied himself with the cultivation of the trees in it, while Blanquerna left the church to recreate his mind which was wearied by the work he had done, to lift his eyes to the hills, and to let them rest on the plains beneath. Feeling rested at last, he would betake himself again to meditation and prayer, and the reading of Holy Scripture or the great book of *Contemplation,* and so he would be occupied until the hours of Terce, Sext and Nones. . . . After this he dined . . . and went into the garden, visited the spring, or walked in the places he loved most, afterwards giving himself up for a while to sleep in order to gather strength for the labours of the night. On awaking he said vespers with the deacon, and then remained alone, thinking on what pleased him most and was fittest preparation for his hours of prayer. After sunset, he went up to the terrace, and there remained long in devout meditation, his eyes fixed on the heavens and the stars, discoursing with himself on the greatness of God and man's inconstancies. In this state he remained until he retired to rest, and such was the fervour of his contemplation that even upon his bed he found himself in mystic converse with the All-Powerful.

Such a background as this we must almost of necessity assume in a life at once so active and so spiritual. No doubt Lull was able often to spend weeks, or at the least days, in some sacred retreat, and draw from God and from Nature strength and inspiration for his endless tasks. To these seasons of refreshing, it may be supposed, we owe his mystical writings.

Of Lull's verses many are narrative or doctrinal : the hymns entitled ' Hours of Our Lady St. Mary ' (*Horas de Nostra Dona Sancta Maria*), for example ; the ' Sin of Adam ' (*Lo Peccat de n'Adam*), written ' at the request of the King of Majorca ' ; the short ' Song of Ramón ' (*Lo Cant de Ramón*), and above all the ' Medicine for Sin ' (*Medicina de Peccat*) and

the purely didactic verse ' Application ' of the *Art
General*.   The collection of a hundred songs on the
Names of God (*Els Cent Noms de Deu*), on the other
hand, is more mystical than doctrinal, and suggests,
in matter as well as in title, the mystical treatise ' Of
the Names of Christ ' (*De los Nombres de Cristo*)
written almost exactly three hundred years later by
the Salamancan friar, Luis de León.   Mystical
too, as well as autobiographical, is the dialogue
poem *El Desconort*, ' made in his old age,' though
its spirit is that of disillusion at the refusal of those
in high places to help forward his schemes of
evangelisation.   But neither of these has either
the strength or the beauty of the collection of prose
poems here translated, a collection which forms
part of the novel-like *Blanquerna*, Lull's chief contribution to mystical literature.

His chief contribution it is, mainly, though not
entirely, by virtue of the sections entitled the *Art
of Contemplation* and our *Book of the Lover and the
Beloved*.   *Blanquerna*, as a whole, is a somewhat
fantastic, and in places extravagant, religious romance—a religious *Utopia*, if parallels to it must
be found, or a Catholic *Pilgrim's Progress*.   The
story is of a certain gallant and wealthy youth named
Evast, who marries a beautiful and virtuous girl
called Aloma.   They live together in great piety
and happiness, but have no children, until Aloma in

her sorrow prays to God, and a boy, Blanquerna, is born to them. The child is brought up with great care, and in the fear of God; and when his father sees that he is a youth of discretion, he resolves to devote himself to the religious life. Aloma, however, disapproves, saying that they can both serve God best in the state to which He has called them; they decide in the end to lead lives of greater austerity in their home, and to give Blanquerna the oversight of the household. But, on proposing this to the boy, they find that he has resolved to become a hermit.

Aloma is grieved, and endeavours to marry Blanquerna to a beautiful girl called Cana. Blanquerna's reply is to persuade Cana to become a nun, while he himself retires to the desert to carry out his resolve. The story then describes circumstantially and with some prolixity the lives of Evast and Aloma after Blanquerna has left them; it passes on to Cana, who eventually becomes abbess of her convent; and finally, after some long digressions upon convent life, to the later history of Blanquerna, which occupies the rest of the romance.

The second book of *Blanquerna* deals with the hero's life before he is ordained priest and rises to the rank of abbot in the monastery which he has entered. A digression follows, entitled ' The Book of Ave Maria,' purporting to be an account of the devotions to Our Lady which the hero established. The third book presents him as a bishop, and the fourth as pope.

The various religious ideals presented by Lull in succession lead up to the great ideal of his life : the evangelisation of the world. Blanquerna's supreme aim as pope is to strive ' that all infidels and schismatics may be brought into the union of the Holy Catholic Faith.' His cardinals are quaintly named after the clauses of the *Gloria in Excelsis Deo*, and every clause is expounded so as to illustrate the activity which the Church should show in converting the heathen.

To the court of the Pope comes at length a jester,—one Ramón the Fool,—none other, of course, than Lull himself. ' I would be as a fool,' he says, ' to do reverence and honour to Jesus Christ, and by reason of my exceeding love I would know no measure in my speech.' Thus disguised, the author can write much which he might not otherwise have dared to put into words. And above all he can deliver himself of the shame he feels because the Head of the Church will grant so little aid to those who aim at following Christ's last recorded command to convert all nations.

The story ends with the decision of Blanquerna, the pope now grown old in the service of the Church and the conversion of the heathen, to renounce his high office, retire to a hermitage, and devote his last days to contemplation and prayer. His new life is described in detail, and it is interwoven with this description that we come upon the *Book of the Lover and the Beloved* and the *Art of Contemplation*.

The former is by far the simpler and more appealing of the two, the *Art of Contemplation* being considerably longer and full of doctrinal teaching. It is, nevertheless, still read, less for its didactic passages than for its close relation with the whole romance, its mystical aspect, and in particular its prayers, which are of great beauty. The *Book of the Lover and the Beloved* is mystical throughout. It was written, the author himself declares, ' that the hearts of men might be moved to true contrition, their eyes to abundance of tears, and their wills and understandings to loftier flights in the contemplation of God.' How well it attains its object, and how truly it reflects the mystic's being, the reader must judge.

III

WE have no wish to add to these few notes a lengthy commentary upon the substance of a book which, probably for the first time, is accessible to those who

read only English. Scholars have debated over
Lull's probable debt to sufism, on the one hand,
and, on the other, his influence upon the long line
of mystics who have followed him. There is much
still to be said upon these and other topics, much
that will throw fresh light on Spain and Spanish
mysticism both. But in this essay enough has
been said of Lull's life and works to form the in-
dispensable prelude to his *Book*. For the present,
therefore, we prefer to stand back, and allow Lull's
ardent spirit to work its miracles still. Work them
it surely must. Writing in his native ' catalan-
provenzal,' that he might appeal, not to learned
men, but to the people, by the people he is read still.
He needs none of the ' Expositions,' such as were
written in his own age and as late as the seventeenth
century. Here and there a passage confuses the
modern mind by its mediæval subtleties ; or the
frequent references to the will, understanding, and
memory (so common in most of the mystics) may
puzzle the simple reader until he has learned to
interpret them. But the vast majority of the three
hundred and sixty-six ' verses,' put together to be
read one on each day of the year, may still so be read.
They speak to the twentieth century as clearly,
picturesquely, and forcibly as they spoke to the
thirteenth. Have we perhaps even more need of
their message ?

They speak of elementals. Like his great successors St. Teresa and St. John of the Cross, Lull knows no Master but his Beloved, Jesus Christ; he surpasses them perhaps in this, that he is never unmindful of the world his Beloved came to save. His is no cloistered love. He could never say, with St. John of the Cross, ' Live in the world as though there were in it but God and thy soul.' Ringing for ever in his ears is the Beloved's last command.

Never was ' Love's regal dalmatic ' worn with more grace and fitness than by this 'jester,' this ' fool of love.' It is no compliment to Lull to call him, as the great scholar Menéndez Pelayo does, a ' Spanish Jacopone da Todi.' Jacopone, it is true, sang of love with unsurpassable fervour :

> Amor, amore, tanto tu me fai,
> Amore, amor, che nol posso patire ;
> Amor, amore, tanto me te dai,
> Amor, amore, ben credo morire ;
> Amore, amore, tanto preso m'hai,
> Amor, amore, famme 'n te transire ;
> Amor, dolce languire,
> Amor mio desioso,
> Amor mio delettoso,
> Annegame en amore.

But Lull, who, like Jacopone, owed most of his fervour, under God, to St. Francis, has a note of his own, no less deep, no less pure. His key is perhaps in that eloquent definition, which has been slightly expanded in translation that the full force of every phrase may be felt :

> ' What meanest thou by love ? ' said the Beloved. And the Lover answered : ' It is to bear on one's heart the sacred marks and the sweet words of the Beloved. It is to long for Him with desire and with tears. It is boldness. It is fervour. It is fear. It is the desire for the Beloved above all things. It is that which causes the Lover to grow faint when he hears the Beloved's praises. It is that in which I die daily, and in which is all my will.'

Lull might well have written, as did a late Franciscan, John of the Angels, of the ' Triumphs of the Love of God.'

Love impels him to tread the Mystic Way ' in search of his Beloved.' Much of his *Book*, therefore, deals with the Mystic Life. But it has none of the exclusiveness of the *Living Flame of Love* and the *Spiritual Canticle*. There are passages for the beginner as well as for the proficient, parables in three lines for the plain man, sermons in phrases, reflections which, by their very simplicity, kindle the devotion of the wayfaring man as he reads them. As we read the brief records of imaginary conversations between the Lover and ' those who asked him concerning his Beloved,' we can imagine ourselves in some African coast-town where the stranger who has just landed is being pressed, by the surging crowd which surrounds him, to give reasons for his faith. The calm and confident answers supply the secret of Lull's power.

Then we come upon some quaintly-worded, paradoxical phrase which only reflection will illumine and meditation make real. And we know that we are following in the path of Lull when he composed his treatise. For it was the fruit, not of subtleties, but of silence. ' He would engage in prayer,' runs the preface, ' and meditate upon God and His virtues, after which he would write down the outcome of his contemplation.' And again, more concretely : ' At midnight he arose, looked out upon the heavens and the stars, and cast away from him all thoughts of the world.'

So, between meditation and prayer, he wrote this masterpiece in little, signed it with his Beloved's Sign, and sent it out to a world which he longed to save. It has been potent in the past, and we may believe that it will be so again. For it is as eternal and universal in its appeal as the Ideal Life which it extols. Nurtured by experience, watered by faith, it is rooted and grounded in love.

THE BOOK OF THE LOVER
AND THE BELOVED

1 The Lover asked his Beloved if there remained in Him anything still to be loved. And the Beloved replied that he had still to love that by which his own love could be increased.

2 Long and perilous are the paths by which the Lover seeks his Beloved. They are peopled by cares, sighs and tears. They are lit up by love.

3 Many Lovers came together to love One only, their Beloved, who made them all to abound in love. And each declared his Beloved perfection, and his thoughts of Him were very pleasant, making him to suffer pain which brought delight.

4 The Lover wept and said : ' How long shall it be till the darkness of the world is past, that the mad rush of men towards hell may cease ? When comes the hour in which water, that flows downwards, shall change its nature and mount upwards ? When shall the innocent be more in number than the guilty ? Ah ! When shall the Lover with joy lay down his life for the Beloved ? And when shall the Beloved see the Lover grow faint for love of Him ? '

5 Said the Lover to the Beloved : ' Thou that fillest the sun with splendour, fill my heart with love.' And the Beloved answered : ' Wert thou

not filled with love, thine eyes had not shed those tears, nor hadst thou come to this place to see thy Beloved.'

6 The Beloved made trial of His Lover to see if his love for Him were perfect, and He asked him how the presence of the Beloved differed from His absence. The Lover answered: 'As knowledge and remembrance differ from ignorance and oblivion.'

7 The Beloved asked the Lover: 'Hast thou remembrance of anything with which I have rewarded thee, that thou wouldst love Me thus?' 'Yea,' replied the Lover, 'for I distinguish not between the trials that Thou sendest me and the joys.'

8 'Say, O Lover,' asked the Beloved, 'if I double thy trials, wilt thou still be patient?' 'Yea,' answered the Lover, 'so that Thou double also my love.'

9 Said the Beloved to the Lover: 'Knowest thou yet what love meaneth?' The Lover replied: 'If I knew not the meaning of love, I should know the meaning of labour, grief and sorrow.'

10 They asked the Lover: 'Why answerest thou not thy Beloved when He calleth thee?' He re-

plied : ' I brave great perils that He may come, and I speak to Him begging His graces.'

11 ' Foolish Lover, why doſt thou weary thy body, throw away thy wealth and leave the joys of this world, and go about as an outcaſt of the people ? ' ' To honour my Beloved's Name,' he replied, ' for He is hated and dishonoured by more men than honour and love Him.'

12 ' Say, Fool of Love, which can be the better seen, the Beloved in the Lover, or the Lover in the Beloved ? ' The Lover answered, and said : ' By love can the Beloved be seen, and the Lover by sighs and tears, by grief and by labours.'

13 The Lover sought for one who should tell his Beloved how great trials he was enduring for love of Him, and how he was like to die. And he found his Beloved, who was reading in a book wherein were written all the griefs which love made him to suffer for his Beloved, and the graces which He gave him.

14 Our Lady presented her Son to the Lover, that he might kiss His feet, and that he might write in his book concerning Our Lady's virtues.

15 ' Say, thou bird that singeſt, haſt thou placed thyself in the care of my Beloved, that He may

guard thee from indifference, and increase in thee thy love?' The bird replied: 'And who makes me to sing but the Lord of love, to whom not to love is to sin.'

16 Between Hope and Fear, Love made her home. She lives on thought, and, when she is forgotten, dies. So unlike the pleasures of this world are her foundations.

17 There was a contention between the eyes and the memory of the Lover, for the eyes said that it was better to see the Beloved than to remember Him. But Memory said that remembrance brings tears to the eyes, and makes the heart to burn with love.

18 The Lover asked the Understanding and the Will which of them was the nearer to his Beloved. And the two ran, and the Understanding came nearer to the Beloved than did the Will.

19 There was strife between the Lover and the Beloved, and another who loved Him saw it and wept, till peace and concord were made between the Beloved and the Lover.

20 Sighs and Tears came to be judged by the Beloved, and asked Him which of them loved Him the more deeply. And the Beloved gave judgment

that sighs were nearer to the seat of love, and tears to the eyes.

21 The Lover came to drink of the fountain which gives love to him who has none, and his griefs redoubled. And the Beloved came to drink of the same fountain, that the love of one whose griefs were doubled might be doubled also.

22 The Lover fell sick and thought on the Beloved, who fed him on His merits, quenched his thirst with love, made him to rest in patience, clothed him with humility, and as medicine gave him truth.

23 They asked the Lover where his Beloved was. And he answered: ' See Him for yourselves in a nobler house than all the nobility of creation ; but see Him too in my love, my griefs and my tears.'

24 They said to the Lover : ' Whither goest thou ? ' He answered : ' I come from my Beloved.' ' Whence comest thou ? ' ' I go to my Beloved.' ' When wilt thou return ? ' ' I shall be with my Beloved.' ' How long wilt thou be with thy Beloved ? ' ' As long as my thoughts remain on Him.'

25 The birds hymned the dawn, and the Beloved, who is the dawn, awakened. And the birds ended their song, and the Lover died in the dawn for his Beloved.

27

26 The bird sang in the garden of the Beloved. The Lover came, and he said to the bird : ' If we understand not one another's speech, we may make ourselves understood by love ; for in thy song I see my Beloved before mine eyes.'

27 The Lover was wearied, for he had laboured much in seeking for his Beloved ; and he feared lest he should forget Him. And he wept, that he might not fall asleep, and his Beloved be absent from his remembrance.

28 The Lover and the Beloved met, and the Beloved said to the Lover : ' Thou needest not to speak to Me. Look at Me only,—for thine eyes speak to My heart,—that I may give thee what thou willest.'

29 The Lover was disobedient to his Beloved ; and the Lover wept. And the Beloved came in the vesture of His Lover, and died, that His Lover might regain what he had lost. So He gave him a greater gift than that which he had lost.

30 The Beloved filled His Lover with gifts of love, and grieved not for his tribulations, for they would but make him love the more deeply ; and the greater the Lover's tribulations, the greater was his joy and delight.

31   The Lover said : ' The secrets of my Beloved torture me, for my deeds reveal them not, and my mouth keeps silence and reveals them to none.'

32   This is Love's contract : the Lover must be long-suffering, patient, humble, fearful, diligent, trustful ; he must be ready to face great dangers for the honour of his Beloved.   And his Beloved is pledged to be true and free, just and liberal with those that love Him.

33   The Lover set forth over hill and plain in search of true devotion, and to see if his Beloved was well served.   But everywhere he found nought but indifference.   And so he delved into the earth to see if there he could find the devotion which was lacking above ground.

34   ' Say, thou bird that singest of love, why does my Beloved, He who has made me His servant, do nought but torture me now ? '   And the bird replied : ' If Love made thee not to bear trials, what couldst thou give to show thy love for Him ? '

35   Pensively the Lover trod those paths which lead to the Beloved.   Now he stumbled and fell among the thorns ; but they were to him as flowers, and as a bed of love.

36   They asked the Lover : ' Wilt thou for another

change thy Beloved?' And he answered: 'Why, what other is better or nobler than He? For He is the supreme Good; He is infinite and eternal, in greatness, wisdom and love; nay, He is perfection.'

37   The Lover wept, and sang of his Beloved, and said: ' Swifter is love in the lover's heart than is the brilliance of the lightning to the eye, or the thunder to the ear. The tears of love gather more swiftly than the waves of the sea; and sighing is more proper to love than is whiteness to snow.'

38   They asked the Lover: ' Wherein is the glory of thy Beloved?' He answered: 'He is Glory itself.' They asked him: 'Wherein lies His power?' He answered: 'He is Power itself.' 'And wherein lies His wisdom?' 'He is Wisdom itself.' 'And wherefore is He to be loved?' 'Because He is Love itself.'

39   The Lover rose early and went to seek his Beloved. He found travellers on the road, and he asked if they had seen his Beloved. They answered him: ' When did the eyes of thy mind lose sight of thy Beloved?' The Lover replied: 'Since I first saw my Beloved in my thoughts, He has never been absent from the eyes of my body, for all things that I see picture to me my Beloved.'

40   With eyes of thought and grief, sighs and tears the Lover gazed upon the Beloved ; and with eyes of grace, justice and piety, mercy and bounty, the Beloved gazed upon His Lover. And the bird sang of that Countenance so full of delight, as we have already said.

41   The keys of the gates of love are gilded with cares and desires, sighs and tears ; the cord which binds them is woven of conscience, devotion, contrition and atonement ; the door is kept by justice and mercy.

42   The Lover beat upon his Beloved's door with blows of love and hope. The Beloved heard His Lover's blows, with humility, piety, charity and patience. Deity and Humanity opened the doors, and the Lover went in to his Beloved.

43   Deity and Humanity met, and joined together to make concord between Lover and Beloved.

44   There are two fires that warm the love of a true Lover : one is of pleasures, desires and thoughts : the other is of weeping and crying, of fear and grief.

45   The Lover longed for solitude, and went away to live alone, that he might gain the companionship of his Beloved, for amid many people he was lonely.

46   The Lover was all alone, in the shade of a great tree. Men passed by that place, and asked him why

he was alone. And the Lover replied : ' I am alone, now that I have seen you and heard you ; until now, I was in the company of my Beloved.'

47 By signs of love, the Lover held converse with the Beloved ; by means of fear and thought, weeping and crying, the Lover recounted his griefs to the Beloved.

48 The Lover feared whether his Beloved would fail him in his greatest need ; and he ceased from loving Him. Then he had contrition and repentance of heart ; and the Beloved restored hope and charity to the Lover's heart, and tears to his eyes, that love might return to him.

49 Whether Lover and Beloved are near or far is all one ; for their love mingles as water mingles with wine. They are linked as heat with light ; they approach and are united as Essence and Being.

50 Said the Lover to the Beloved : ' My grief and its healing are both in Thee : the more surely Thou healest me, the greater grows my grief ; when Thou dost wound me, even then dost Thou give me health.'

51 The Lover sighed and said : ' Ah ! What is my love ? ' The Beloved answered : ' Thy love is a mark and a seal by which thou dost show forth My honour before men.'

52 The Lover saw himself taken and bound, wounded and killed, for the love of his Beloved ; and those who tortured him asked him : ' Where is thy Beloved ? ' He answered : ' See Him here in the increase of my love, and the strength which it gives me to bear my torments.'

53 Said the Lover to the Beloved : ' I have never fled from Thee, nor ceased to love Thee, since I knew Thee, for I was ever in Thee, by Thee and with Thee wheresoever I went.' The Beloved answered : ' Nor since thou hast known Me and loved Me have I once forgotten thee ; never once have I deceived or failed thee.'

54 As though mad went the Lover through a city, singing of his love ; and they asked him if he had lost his senses. ' My Beloved,' he answered, ' has taken my will, and I myself have yielded up to Him my understanding ; so that there is left in me naught but memory, with which I remember my Beloved.'

55 The Beloved said : ' It would be a miracle that the Lover should sleep and forget the love of the Beloved.' The Lover replied : ' It would be a greater miracle yet if the Beloved did not awaken him, since He has desired his love.'

56 The heart of the Lover soared to the heights of

the Beloved's abode, so that he might not lose his
love for Him in the deep places of this world. And
when he reached his Beloved he contemplated Him
with joy and delight. But the Beloved led him
down again to this world to make trial of him with
tribulations and adversities.

57 They asked the Lover : 'Wherein is all thy
wealth ? ' He answered : ' In the poverty which
I bear for my Beloved.' 'And where dost thou
rest ? ' ' In the afflictions of love.' 'Who is thy
physician ? ' 'The trust I have in my Beloved.'
' And who is thy master ? ' ' The signs which in
all creatures I see of my Beloved.'

58 The bird sang upon a branch in leaf and flower,
and the breeze caused the leaves to tremble, and
bore away the scent of the flowers. 'What means
the trembling of the leaves, and the scent of
the flowers ? ' asked the bird of the Lover.
He answered : ' The trembling of the leaves
signifies obedience, and the scent of the flowers,
adversity.'

59 The Lover went in desire of his Beloved and
met two friends, who greeted each other lovingly,
with kisses, embraces and tears. And the Lover
swooned, so strongly did these two lovers call to his
memory his Beloved.

60　The Lover thought on death, and was afraid, till he remembered his Beloved. Then in a loud voice he cried to those who were near : ' Ah, sirs ! have love, that you may fear neither death nor danger, in doing honour to my Beloved.'

61　They asked the Lover where his love first began. And he replied : ' It began in the glory of my Beloved ; and from that beginning I was led to love my neighbour even as myself, and to cease to care for deception and falsehood.'

62　' Say, Fool of Love, if thy Beloved no longer cared for thee, what wouldst thou do ? ' ' I should love Him still,' he replied. ' Else must I die ; seeing that to cease to love is death and love is life.'

63　They asked the Lover what he meant by perseverance. ' It is both happiness and sorrow,' he answered, ' in the Lover who ever loves, honours and serves his Beloved with courage, patience and hope.'

64　The Lover desired his Beloved to recompense him for the time of his service. And the Beloved reckoned the thoughts, tears, longings, perils and trials which His Lover had borne for love of Him ; and the Beloved added to the account eternal bliss, and gave Himself for a recompense to His Lover.

65　They asked the Lover what he meant by

happiness. ' It is sorrow,' he replied, ' borne for
Love's sake.' ' O Fool,' they answered, ' what,
then, is sorrow ? ' ' It is the remembrance of dishonour done to my Beloved, who is worthy of all
honour.' And they asked him again : ' What is
misery ? ' ' To get one's desires in this world,'
he replied, ' for such fleeting joys are followed by
perpetual torment.'

66   The Lover was gazing on a Place where he had
seen his Beloved.   And he said : ' Ah, place that
recallest the blessed haunts of my Beloved !   Thou
wilt tell my Beloved that I suffer trials and griefs for
His sake.'   And that Place made reply : ' When thy
Beloved hung upon me, He bore for thy love
greater trials and sorrows than all other trials and
sorrows that Love could give to its servants.'

67   Said the Lover to his Beloved : ' Thou art all,
and through all, and in all, and with all.   I would
give Thee all of myself that I may have all of Thee,
and Thou all of me.'   The Beloved answered :
' Thou canst not have Me wholly unless thou art
wholly Mine.'   And the Lover said : ' Let me be
wholly Thine and be Thou wholly mine.'   The
Beloved answered : ' If I am wholly thine, what
part in Me will thy son have, thy brother, thy sister
and thy father ? '   The Lover replied : ' Thou, O
my Beloved ! art so great a Whole, that Thou canst

abound, and yet be wholly of each one who gives himself wholly to Thee.'

68 The Lover thought long and deeply on the greatness and everlastingness of his Beloved, and he found in Him neither beginning, nor mean, nor end. And the Beloved said : ' What art thou measuring, O Fool ? ' The Lover answered : ' I am measuring greater with lesser, fullness with want, infinity with quantity, and eternity with time. And this I do that humility and patience, faith, love and hope may enter more deeply into my mind.'

69 The paths of love are both long and short. For love is clear, pure and bright, subtle yet simple, strong, diligent, brilliant, and abounding both in fresh thoughts and in old memories.

70 They asked the Lover : ' What are the fruits of love ? ' And the Lover made answer : ' They are pleasures, thoughts, desires, trials, perils, torments, sighs and griefs. And without these fruits Love's servants have no part in her.'

71 Many persons were with the Lover, who was complaining of his Beloved that He increased not his love, and of Love, that it gave him so many trials and sorrows. The Beloved made reply that the trials and sorrows for which he reproached Love were that very increase of love.

72   The Lover entered a delightful meadow, and saw in the meadow many children who were pursuing butterflies, and trampling down the flowers ; and, the more the children laboured to catch the butterflies, the higher did these fly.   And the Lover, as he watched them, said : ' Such are they who with subtle reasoning attempt to comprehend the Beloved, Who opens the doors to the simple and closes them to the subtle.   And Faith reveals the secrets of the Beloved through the casement of love.'

73   ' Say, Fool of Love, why dost thou not speak, and what is this for which thou art thoughtful and perplexed ? '   The Lover answered : ' I am thinking of the beauties of my Beloved, and the likeness between the bliss and the sorrow which are brought me by the gifts of Love.'

74   ' Say, Fool, which was in being first, thy heart or thy love ? '   He answered and said : ' Both came into being together ; for were it not so, the heart had not been made for love, nor love for reflection.'

75   They asked the Fool : ' Where did thy love have its birth : in the secrets of the Beloved, or in the revelation of them ? '   He replied : ' Love in its fullness makes no such distinction as this ; for

38

secretly the Lover hides the secrets of his Beloved;
secretly also he reveals them, and yet when they
are revealed he keeps them secret still.'

76 The secrets of love, unrevealed, cause anguish
and grief; revelation of love brings fervour and fear.
And for this cause the Lover must ever be suffering.

77 Love called his lovers, and bade them ask of
him the most desirable and pleasing gifts. And
they asked of Love that he would clothe and adorn
them after his own manner, that they might be
more acceptable to the Beloved.

78 The Lover cried aloud to all men, and said:
' Love bids you ever love: in walking and sitting,
in sleeping and waking, in buying and selling, in
weeping and laughing, in speech and in silence, in
gain and in loss—in short, in whatsoever you do,
for this is Love's commandment.'

79 ' Say, Fool, when did Love first come to thee?'
' In that time,' he replied, ' when my heart was
filled and enriched with thoughts and desires, sighs
and griefs, and my eyes with tears.' ' And what did
Love bring thee?' ' The wondrous ways of my
Beloved, His honours and His exceeding worth.'
' How did these things come?' ' Through my
memory and understanding.' ' How didst thou
receive them?' ' With love and hope.' ' How

dost thou keep them?' 'With justice and prudence, temperance and courage.'

80   The Beloved sang, and said : ' Little the Lover knows of love, if he is ashamed to praise his Beloved, or if he fears to do Him honour in that place where He is most dishonoured ; and little has he learned to love who is impatient of tribulations; and he who loses trust in his Beloved loses also his love and hope.'

81   The Lover wrote to his Beloved, and asked Him if there were others who could help him to suffer and bear the grievous trials which he endured for love of Him. And the Beloved replied to the Lover : ' There is nought in Me that can forsake nor fail thee.'

82   They asked the Beloved concerning the love of His Lover. He answered : ' It is a mingling of joy and sorrow, of fervency and fear.' They asked the Lover concerning the love of his Beloved. And he answered : ' It is the inflowing of infinite goodness, eternal life, power, wisdom, charity and perfection. This is that which flows to the Lover from the Beloved.'

83   ' Say, O Fool, what meanest thou by a marvel ? ' He replied : ' It is a marvel to love things absent more than things present ; and no less to love things

seen and things corruptible more than things unseen and incorruptible.'

84 The Lover went to seek his Beloved, and he found a man who was dying without love. And he said : ' How great a sadness is it that any man should die without love ! ' So the Lover said to him that was dying : ' Say, why dost thou die without love ? ' And he replied : ' Because I lived without love.'

85 The Lover asked his Beloved : ' Which is the greater—loving, or love itself ? ' The Beloved answered : ' In this mortal life, love is the tree, the fruit of which is loving ; the flowers and the leaves are trials and griefs. And in God, love and loving are one and the same thing, without either griefs or trials.'

86 The Lover was sorrowful, and wearied with overmuch thought. And therefore he begged his Beloved to send him a book, in which he might see Him in His virtues, that his sorrow might thereby be relieved. So the Beloved sent that book to the Lover, and his trials and griefs were doubled.

87 Sick with love was the Lover, and a physician came in to see him who doubled his sorrows and his thoughts. And in that same hour the Lover was healed.

88 Love went apart with the Lover, and they had great joy of the Beloved as they communed of Him. The Lover wept, and afterwards was in rapture, and Love swooned thereat. But the Beloved brought life to His Lover by revealing to him His Countenance.

89 The Lover said to the Beloved : ' By many ways doſt Thou come to my heart, and revealeſt Thyself to my sight. And by many names do I name Thee. But the love by which Thou suſtaineſt me and humbleſt me is one, and one alone.'

90 The Beloved revealed Himself to His Lover, clothed in new and scarlet robes. He stretched out His Arms to embrace him ; He inclined His Head to kiss him ; and He remained on high that he might ever seek Him.

91 The Beloved was absent from His Lover, and the Lover sought his Beloved with his memory and underſtanding, that he might worthily love Him. The Lover found his Beloved, and asked Him whither He had been. ' Far from thy memory,' answered the Beloved, 'and in a place which thy underſtanding knew not.'

92 ' Say, O Fool, haſt thou shame when men see thee weep for thy Beloved ? ' ' Shame apart from sin,' answered the Lover, ' signifies want of love in one who knows not how to love.'

93   The Beloved planted in the heart of the Lover sighs and longings, virtue and love. The Lover watered the seed with his tears. In the body of the Lover the Beloved planted trials, tribulations and griefs. And the Lover tended his body with hope and devotion, consolation and patience.

94   The Beloved made a great feaſt, gathered an assembly of many noble knights, sent many invitations and gave great gifts. To this assembly came the Lover, and the Beloved said to him : ' Who called thee to come to this assembly ? ' The Lover answered : ' Need and love compelled me to come, that I might behold Thy face, Thy wonders, Thy adornments and Thy glory.'

95   They asked the Lover : ' Whence art thou ? ' He answered : ' From love.'   ' To whom doſt thou belong ? '   ' I belong to love.'   ' Who gave thee birth ? '   ' Love.'   ' Where waſt thou born ? '   ' In love.'   ' Who brought thee up ? '   ' Love.'   ' How doſt thou live ? '   ' By love.'   ' What is thy name ? '   ' Love.'   ' Whence comeſt thou ? '   ' From love.'   ' Whither goeſt thou ? '   ' To love.'   ' Where dwelleſt thou ? '   ' In love.'   ' Haſt thou aught but love ? '   ' Yea,' he answered, ' I have faults ; and I have sins againſt my Beloved.'   ' Is there pardon in thy Beloved ? '   ' Yea,' answered the Lover, ' in my Beloved there is juſtice and

43

mercy, and therefore am I lodged between fear and hope ; for mercy causes me to hope and justice to fear.'

96 The Beloved left the Lover, and the Lover sought Him in his thoughts, and inquired for Him of men in the language of love. The Lover found his Beloved, who was despised among the people, and he told the Beloved what great wrong was done to His Name. The Beloved answered him, and said : ' Lo, I suffer these wrongs for want of fervent and devoted lovers.' The Lover wept, and his sorrow was increased, but the Beloved comforted him, by revealing to him His Presence.

97 The light of the Beloved's abode came to illumine the Lover's dwelling, which was full of darkness, and to fill it with joy, with grief and with thoughts. And the Lover cast out all things from his dwelling, that the Beloved might be lodged there.

98 They asked the Lover what sign the Beloved bore upon His banner. He replied : ' The sign of One dead.' They asked him why He bore such a sign. He answered : ' Because He was once crucified, and was dead, and because those who glory in being His lovers must follow His steps.'

99 The Beloved came to lodge in the dwelling of His Lover, and the steward demanded of Him the

reckoning. But the Lover said : ' My Beloved is to be lodged freely,—yea, with a gift,—for long ago He paid the price of all men.'

100 Memory and Will met together, and climbed into the mountain of the Beloved, that understanding might be exalted and love for the Beloved might be increased.

101 Every day sighs and tears are messengers between the Lover and the Beloved, that between them there may be solace and companionship, love and goodwill.

102 The Lover desired his Beloved, and sent to Him his thoughts, that they might bring him back from his Beloved the joys which for so long had been his.

103 The Beloved gave to His Lover the gift of tears, sighs, thoughts, weariness and grief, with which gift the Lover served his Beloved.

104 The Lover begged his Beloved to give him riches, peace and honour in this world ; and the Beloved revealed His Countenance to the memory and understanding of the Lover, and gave Himself as the Supreme Aim to his will.

105 They asked the Lover : ' In what consists honour ? ' He answered : ' In comprehending and

45

loving my Beloved.' And they asked him also : ' In what consists dishonour ? ' He answered : ' In forgetting and ceasing to love Him.'

106 ' O my Beloved, I was tormented by love, until I cried that Thou wast present in my torments ; and then did love ease my griefs, and Thou as a guerdon didst increase my love, even as Thou didst double my torment.'

107 In the path of love the Lover found another who was silent, and who with tears, grief, and a sad countenance made accusation and reproach against Love. And Love made excuse, saying that he had given him noble gifts : loyalty, hope, patience, devotion, courage, temperance and happiness ; and he blamed the Lover who cried out upon Love, for that he had given him such gifts as these.

108 The Lover sang and said : ' Ah, what great affliction is love ! Ah, what great happiness it is to love my Beloved, who loves His lovers with infinite and eternal love, perfect and complete in everything!'

109 The Lover went into a far country seeking his Beloved, and in the way he met two lions. The Lover was afraid, even to death, for he desired to live and serve his Beloved. So he sent Memory to his Beloved, that Love might be present at his passing, for with Love he could better endure death.

And while the Lover thought upon his Beloved, the two lions came humbly to the Lover, licked the tears from his eyes, and caressed his hands and feet. So the Lover went on his way in search of his Beloved.

110 The Lover journeyed over hill and dale, but he could find no way of escape from the imprisonment in which Love had for so long enthralled his body and his thoughts and all his desires and joys. While the Lover went labouring thus, he found a hermit who was sleeping near to a fair spring. The Lover wakened the hermit, and asked him if in his dreams he had seen the Beloved. The hermit replied that his own thoughts also, whether he was sleeping or waking, were imprisoned by Love. And the Lover joyed greatly at finding a fellow-prisoner ; so they both wept, for the Beloved has few such lovers as these.

111 There is naught in the Beloved which is not care and sorrow for the Lover, nor has the Lover aught in himself in which the Beloved joys not and has no part. And therefore is the love of the Beloved ever active, while that of the Lover is grief and suffering.

112 A bird was singing upon a branch : ' I will give a fresh thought to the lover who will give me

two.' The bird gave that fresh thought to the Lover, and the Lover gave two to the bird, that its grief might be assuaged; and the Lover felt his griefs increased.

113 The Lover and the Beloved met together, and their caresses and embraces, their weeping and crying, bore witness to their meeting. Then the Beloved asked the Lover concerning his state, and the Lover was speechless before his Beloved.

114 The Lover and the Beloved strove, and their love made peace between them. Which of them, think you, bore the stronger love toward the other?

115 The Lover loved all who feared his Beloved, and he feared all who feared Him not. And there arose this doubt: Had the Lover more of love or of fear?

116 The Lover thought to follow his Beloved, and he passed along a road where there was a fierce lion which killed all who passed by it carelessly and without devotion. Then the Lover said: 'He who fears not my Beloved must fear everything, and he who fears Him may be bold and fervent in all things beside.'

117 They asked the Lover: 'What meanest thou by occasion of love?' He answered: 'It is to have

pleasure in penance, understanding in knowledge, hope in patience, health in abstinence, consolation in remembrance, love in diligence, loyalty in destitution, riches in poverty, peace in obedience, strife in malevolence.'

118 Love shone through the cloud which came between the Lover and the Beloved, and made it as bright and resplendent as is the moon by night, as the day-star at dawn, the sun at midday, the understanding in the will; and through that bright cloud the Lover and the Beloved held converse.

119 They asked the Lover : ' What is the greatest darkness ? ' He replied : ' The absence of my Beloved.' ' And what is the greatest light ? ' ' The presence of my Beloved.'

120 The marks of the Beloved are seen in the Lover, who for love's sake is in thought and grief, sighs and tears, and contempt of the people.

121 The Lover wrote these words : ' My Beloved delighteth because I raise my thoughts to Him, and my eyes are in grief and tears, and I neither live nor feel, nor taste nor see nor hear.'

122 Ah, understanding and will, cry out and awaken the watchdogs who sleep, forgetting my Beloved. Weep, O eyes ! Sigh, O heart ! And,

E

memory, forget not the dishonour which is done to my Beloved by those whom He has so greatly honoured.

123   The enmity of men to my Beloved increases. Yet my Beloved promises gifts and rewards, and threatens with justice and wisdom. And memory and will despise both His threats and His promises.

124   The Beloved drew near to the Lover, to comfort and console him for the grief which he suffered and the tears which he shed.   And the nearer was the Lover to the Beloved, the more he grieved and wept, crying out upon the dishonour which his Beloved endured.

125   With the pen of love, with the water of his tears, and on paper of suffering, the Lover wrote letters to his Beloved.   And in these he told how devotion tarried, how love was dying, and how falsehood and error were increasing the number of His enemies.

126   The Lover and the Beloved were bound in love with the bonds of memory, understanding, and will, that they might never be parted ; and the cord with which these two loves were bound was woven of thoughts and griefs, sighs and tears.

127   The Lover lay in the bed of love : his sheets were of joy, his coverlet was of griefs, his pillow of tears.   And none knew if the fabric of the pillow was that of the sheets or of the coverlet.

128   The Beloved clothed His Lover in vest, coat and mantle, and gave him a helmet of love.   His body He clothed with thoughts, his feet with tribulations, and his head with a garland of tears.

129   The Beloved adjured His Lover not to forget Him. The Lover replied that he could not forget Him because he could not do otherwise than know Him.

130   The Beloved said to His Lover : ' Thou shalt praise and defend Me in places where men fear to praise Me.'   The Lover answered : ' Provide me then with love.'   The Beloved answered : ' For love of thee I became incarnate, and endured the pains of death.'

131   The Lover said to his Wellbeloved : ' Teach me how to make Thee known and loved and praised among men.'   The Beloved filled His Lover with devotion, patience, charity, tribulations, thoughts, sighs and tears.   And boldness to praise the Beloved entered the Lover's heart ; and in his mouth were praises of his Beloved ; and in his will was contempt of the murmurings of men who judge falsely.

132 The Lover said to the people : ' He who truly remembers my Beloved, in remembering Him forgets all things around ; and he who forgets all things in remembering my Beloved, is defended by Him from all harm, and receives a part in all His blessings.'

133 They asked the Lover : ' Whereof is Love born, whereon does it live, and wherefore does it die ? ' The Lover answered : ' Love is born of remembrance, it lives on understanding, it dies through forgetfulness.'

134 The Lover forgot all that was beneath the high heavens that his understanding might soar the higher towards a knowledge of the Beloved, whom his will desired to comprehend, to contemplate, praise and preach.

135 The Lover went to the wars for the honour of his Beloved, and took with him faith, hope and charity, justice, prudence, strength and temperance with which to vanquish his Beloved's enemies. And the Lover would have been vanquished if the Beloved had not helped him to make known His greatness.

136 The Lover desired to attain to the farthest goal of his love for the Beloved ; and other objects blocked his path. For this cause his longing desires and thoughts gave the Lover sorrow and grief.

137   The Lover was glad, and rejoiced in the greatness of his Beloved.   But afterwards the Lover was sad because of overmuch thought and reflection. And he knew not which he felt the more deeply—the joys or the sorrows.

138   The Lover was sent by his Beloved to Christian princes and to unbelievers, to teach them by his *Art* [1] and his *Elements* [1] to know and love his Beloved.

139   If thou seest a lover clothed in fine raiment, prizing vainglory, sated with food and sleep, know that in that man thou seest damnation and torment. And if thou seest a lover poorly clothed, despised by the world, pale and thin with fast and vigil, know that in that man thou lookest upon salvation and everlasting weal.

140   The Lover made complaint to his Beloved of the heat of the fire which raged in his breast.   The Lover was like to die, and the Beloved wept, and gave him the comfort of patience and the sure hope of reward.

141   The Lover wept for all that he had lost; and none could comfort him, for his losses could not be regained.

[1] Works of Lull himself.

142 God created the night that men might keep vigil, and meditate upon the glories of the Beloved: there was a time when the Lover thought that it was created for the rest and sleep of those who were wearied with loving.

143 Men reproached and reproved the Lover, because he went about as a fool for love's sake. And the Lover despised their reproaches, and himself reproved them, because they loved not his Beloved.

144 The Lover said : ' I am clothed in vile raiment; but love clothes my heart with thoughts of delight, and my body with tears, griefs and sufferings.'

145 The Beloved sang, and said : ' I taught those who praise Me to sing My praises aright, and the enemies of My honour have tormented and despised them. Therefore have I sent my Lover that he may weep and lament the dishonour which I have suffered, and his laments and tears are the fruit of My love.'

146 The Lover made oath to the Beloved that for love of Him he endured and loved trials and sufferings, and he begged the Beloved that He would think upon his trials and sufferings. The Beloved made oath that it was the nature and property of His love to love all those that loved Him, and to have pity on those who endured trials for love of Him.

The Lover was glad, and rejoiced in the nature and property of his Beloved.

147   The Beloved silenced His Lover, and the Lover took comfort in gazing upon his Beloved.

148   The Lover wept and called upon his Beloved, until the Beloved came down from the heights of Heaven ; and He came to earth to weep and suffer and die for the sake of love, and to teach men to know and love and praise His Name.

149   The Lover reproached Christian people, because in their letters they put not first the name of his Beloved, Jesus Christ, to do Him the same honour that the Saracens do to the false prophet Mahomet, when they honour him by naming him before everything in their letters.

150   The Lover met a Squire, pale, thin, and poorly clothed, who was walking along in pensive fashion ; and he saluted the Lover and said : ' Now God guide thee, that thou mayest find thy Beloved ! ' And the Lover asked him how he had recognised him ; and the Squire said : ' Some of Love's secrets reveal others, and therefore between lovers there is recognition.'

151   The glory, honour and goodness of the Beloved are the riches and treasure of the Lover.   And the

Beloved's treasure is the store of thoughts, desires, torments, tears and griefs with which the Lover ever loves and honours his Beloved.

152   A great and goodly company of tried lovers have gathered together; they bear the banner of love, on which is the form and figure of their Beloved. And they will have with them none who has not love, lest their Beloved should be dishonoured.

153   They who show their folly by heaping up riches move the Lover to be a fool for love; and the shame which the Lover feels at going as a fool among men makes him to be esteemed and loved. Which of the two emotions, think you, is the greater occasion of love?

154   Love made the Lover to be sad through excess of thought; the Beloved sang, and the Lover rejoiced to hear Him. Which of these two causes, think you, increased more the Lover's love?

155   In the secrets of the Lover are revealed the secrets of the Beloved, and in the secrets of the Beloved are revealed the secrets of the Lover. Which of these two secrets, think you, is the greater cause of revelation?

156   They asked the Fool by what signs his Beloved might be known. He answered: 'By mercy and

pity, which are essentially in His Will, without mutation or change.'

157 Such was the love which the Lover had to his Beloved, that he desired the good of all above the good of each, and for his Beloved to be everywhere known and praised, and desired of all the world.

158 Love and Indifference met in a garden, where the Lover and the Beloved were talking in secret. And Love asked Indifference why he had come to that place. 'That the Lover may cease to love,' he replied, 'and the Beloved to be honoured.' The words of Indifference were greatly displeasing to the Beloved and the Lover, and their love was increased, that Indifference might be vanquished and destroyed thereby.

159 'Say, O Fool, in which dost thou take the greater pleasure—in loving or in hating?' 'In loving,' he replied, 'for I have only hated that I may the better love.'

160 'Say, O Lover, which dost thou strive to understand the better—falsehood or truth?' He answered: 'Truth.' 'And why so?' 'Because I understand falsehood that I may the better understand truth.'

161   The Lover perceived that he was loved by his Beloved, and he inquired of Him if His love and His mercy were one and the same thing. The Beloved affirmed that in His essence there was no distinction between His love and His mercy. Therefore said the Lover : ' Why, then, does Thy love torment me, and why does not Thy mercy heal me of my griefs ? '

162   The Lover desired to go into a far country to do honour to his Beloved, and he wished to disguise himself that he might not be taken captive on the way ; but he could not hide the tears in his eyes, nor his pale and drawn face, nor the thoughts, complaints and sighs, the sorrow and grief of his heart. And so he was taken captive on the journey and delivered to the tormentors by the enemies of his Beloved.

163   Imprisoned was the Lover in the prison of Love. Thoughts, desires and memories held and enchained him lest he might flee from his Beloved. Griefs tormented him ; patience and hope consoled him. And the Lover was dying, but the Beloved revealed to him His Presence, and the Lover revived.

164   The Lover met his Beloved, and he knew Him and wept. The Beloved reproved him, because he wept not until he knew Him. ' How didst thou know Me,' He asked, ' since thine eyes were not

already wet with tears ? ' And the Lover answered :
' By memory, understanding and will, through which,
as soon as the eyes of my body saw Thee, my love
was increased.'

165 'What meanest thou by love?' said the
Beloved. And the Lover answered : ' It is to bear
on one's heart the sacred marks and the sweet words
of the Beloved. It is to long for Him with desire
and with tears. It is boldness. It is fervour. It
is fear. It is the desire for the Beloved above all
things. It is that which causes the Lover to grow
faint when he hears the Beloved's praises. It is
that in which I die daily, and in which is all my will.'

166 Devotion and Absent Longing sent thoughts
as messengers to the Lover's heart, to bring tears to
his eyes, which for long had wept but now would
weep no more.

167 Said the Lover : ' O ye that love, if ye will
have fire, come light your lanterns at my heart ; if
water, come to my eyes, whence flow the tears in
streams ; if thoughts of love, come gather them
from my meditations.'

168 It happened one day that the Lover was medi-
tating on the great love which he had for his Beloved,
and the great trials and perils into which this love
for so long had led him, and he fell to considering

his reward, which, he said, would surely be great. And as he thus discoursed with himself, it came to him that his Beloved had recompensed him already, for had he not been inspired with a love for His Presence,—with that very love through which his sufferings had come?

169 The Lover was wiping away the tears which for Love's sake he had shed, that none should see the sufferings which the Beloved sent him. But the Beloved said : ' Why wouldst thou hide from others these marks of thy love? Behold, I have given them to thee that others may love and honour Me also.'

170 ' Say, O thou that goest as a fool for love's sake, how long wilt thou be a slave, and forced to weep and suffer trials and griefs?' He answered : ' Till my Beloved shall separate body and soul in me.'

171 ' Say, O Fool, hast thou riches?' He answered : ' I have my Beloved.' ' Hast thou villas, castles or cities, provinces or kingdoms?' He answered : ' I have thoughts of love, tears, desires, trials, griefs, which are better than kingdoms or empires.'

172 They asked the Lover : ' How knowest thou the justice of thy Beloved's decrees?' He answered :

' In that He allots to his lovers an equality of joys and of griefs.'

173 ' Say, O Fool, which of these knows the more of love—he that has joys or he that has trials and griefs?' He answered: ' There can be no knowledge of love without both the one and the other.'

174 They asked the Lover: ' Why wilt thou not defend thyself from the falsehoods, errors and crimes of which thou art accused?' He answered and said: ' I have to defend my Beloved, whom men falsely accuse; man may indeed be full of deceit and error, and is scarce worthy to be defended.'

175 ' Say, O Fool, why defendest thou Love when it thus tries and torments thy body and thy soul?' He answered: ' Because it increases my worth and my happiness.'

176 The Lover grieved and cried out on his Beloved, because He caused Love to torment him so grievously. And the Beloved made reply by increasing his trials and perils, thoughts and tears.

177 ' Say, O Fool, why dost thou excuse the guilty?' He answered: ' That I may not be like those who accuse the innocent with the guilty.'

178 The Beloved raised the understanding of the Lover that he might comprehend His greatness, and

incline his memory to recall his own shortcomings, so that his will might hate them, and aspire to a love of the Beloved and His perfection.

179   The Lover sang of his Beloved and said : ' So great is my will to love Thee, that all I hated once is now, through love of Thee, a greater happiness and joy to me than what I once loved before ever I loved Thee.'

180   The Lover went through a city, and asked if there were none with whom he might speak of his Beloved as he wished. And they showed him a poor man who was weeping for love, and who sought a companion with whom to speak of love.

181   Thoughtful and perplexed was the Lover, as he wondered how his trials could have their source in the glory of his Beloved, who has such great felicity in Himself. And then he thought of the sun, which, though it is so high, strikes the weak eyes of us men that are here below.

182   The thoughts of the Lover were between forgetfulness of his torments and remembrance of his joys ; for the joys of love drive the memory of sorrow away, and the tortures of love recall the happiness which it brings.

183   They asked the Lover : ' Will thy Beloved ever take away thy love ? '   And he answered : ' No, not while memory has power to remember, nor understanding to comprehend the Beloved's glory.'

184   ' Say, O Fool, what is the greatest comparison and similitude of all that can be made ? '   He answered : ' That between Lover and Beloved.' They asked him : ' For what reason ? '   He replied : ' For the greatness of their love.'

185   They asked the Beloved : ' Hast Thou never had pity ? '   He answered : ' If I had not had pity, my Lover had never learned to love Me, nor had I tormented him with sighs and tears, with trials and with griefs.'

186   The Lover was in a vast forest, seeking his Beloved.   He found there Truth and Falsehood, who were disputing of his Beloved, for Truth praised Him and Falsehood accused Him.   And the Lover cried out to Love that he would come to the aid of Truth.

187   There came the temptation to the Lover to leave his Beloved, that memory might awaken and find the Beloved's Presence once more ; that his love should thereby become deeper, that the understanding should comprehend Him more sublimely, and the will love Him more truly.

188 For one day the Lover ceased to remember his Beloved, and on the next day he remembered that he had forgotten Him. On the day when it came to the Lover that he had forgotten his Beloved, he was in sorrow and pain, and yet in glory and bliss, —the one for having forgotten Him, and the other for the joy of the remembrance.

189 So earnestly did the Lover desire that his Beloved should be honoured and praised, that he doubted if he honoured Him enough; and so strongly did he abhor the dishonour paid to his Beloved, that he doubted if he abhorred it enough. And for this cause the Lover was thoughtful, and wavered between love and fear.

190 The Lover was like to die of joy, and he lived by grief. And his joys and torments were mingled and united, and became one and the same thing in the Lover's will. And for this cause the Lover seemed to be living and dying at one and the same time.

191 For one hour only the Lover would fain have forgotten his Beloved, and known Him not, that his grief might have some rest. But such oblivion and ignorance had themselves made him to suffer; therefore he had patience, and lifted up his understanding and his memory, in contemplation of his Beloved.

192 So great was the love of the Lover to his Beloved that he believed all things that He revealed to him. And so earnestly did he desire to comprehend Him that he strove with his reason to understand all things that were said of Him. And therefore was the love of the Lover for ever between belief and understanding.

193 They asked the Lover: 'What thing is farthest from thy heart?' He answered: 'Indifference.' 'And why so?' 'Because nearest to my heart is love, which is the contrary of indifference.'

194 'Say, O Fool, hast thou envy?' He answered: 'Yea, whensoever I forget the bounty and riches of my Beloved.'

195 'Say, O Lover, hast thou riches?' 'Yea,' he replied, 'I have love.' 'Hast thou poverty?' 'Yea, I have love.' 'How then is this?' 'I am poor,' he replied, 'because my love is no greater, and because it fills so few others with love for the honour of my Beloved.'

196 'Say, O Lover, where is thy power?' He answered: 'In the power of my Beloved.' 'Wherewith dost thou fight thine enemies?' 'With the strength of my Beloved.' 'Wherein dost thou seek consolation?' 'In the eternal treasuers of my Beloved.'

197 ' Say, O Fool, which lovest thou the more—
the mercy or the justice of thy Beloved ? ' He
answered : ' So greatly do I love and fear His justice
that I find it not in my will to love anything more.'

198 Sins and merits were striving among themselves in the Lover's conscience. Justice and remembrance increased his remorse, but mercy and
hope increased in his will the assurance of pardon ;
and therefore in the Lover's penitence the merits
conquered the sins.

199 The Lover affirmed that all was perfection in
his Beloved, and denied that in Him was any fault
at all. Which of these two, think you, is the greater
wonder ?

200 There was an eclipse in the heavens and darkness over all the earth. And it recalled to the Lover
that his guilt had separated him long ago from his
Wellbeloved and the darkness had banished the
light from his understanding. This is that light by
which the Beloved reveals Himself to His lovers.

201 Love came to the Lover, who asked him :
' What wilt thou ? ' And Love replied : ' I have
come to thee that I may nurture and direct thy life,
so that at thy death thou shalt be able through my
aid to vanquish thy mortal enemies.'

202   When the Lover forgot his Beloved, Love fell sick ; and when he gave himself to over-much thinking, he himself fell sick, and his Beloved gave him trials, griefs and cares.

203   The Lover found a man who was dying without love. And the Lover wept that a man should die without love, for the dishonour which it brought to his Beloved. So he asked that man : ' Why dost thou die without love ? ' And he answered : ' There is none who will give me knowledge of love, or teach me to be a lover.' So the Lover sighed and wept, and said : ' Ah, devotion, when wilt thou be great enough to drive away sin, and to win for my Beloved many fervent and ardent lovers who will never shrink from praising His Name ? '

204   The Lover tempted Love to see if he would remain in his heart though he remembered not his Beloved ; and his heart ceased to think and his eyes to weep. So his love vanished, and the Lover was perplexed. And he asked all men if they had seen Love.

205   Love and loving, Lover and Beloved are so straitly united in the Beloved, that they are of His Essence, and are one. And this though Lover and Beloved are entities distinct, which agree without diversity of essence. So the Beloved is to be loved above all other objects of affection.

206 ' Say, O Fool, wherefore hast thou so great love ? ' He answered : ' Because long and perilous is the journey which I make in search of my Beloved, and I must seek Him with great faith, and journey with all speed. And none of these things can be accomplished without great love.'

207 The Lover watched and fasted, wept, gave alms, and travelled afar that the Will of the Beloved might be moved to inspire His subjects with love to honour His Name ; but the Lover considered that water does not by nature grow hot, nor mount on high, unless it be first heated. Therefore he prayed the Beloved that He would deign first to warm him in his journeys, alms and vigils with the heat of love, that he might accomplish his desires.

208 The Lover met a pilgrim who sang : ' If the love of the Lover suffices not to move his Beloved to pity and pardon, the love of the Beloved is sufficient to give graces and blessings to His creatures.'

209 ' Say, O Fool, how canst thou be most like to thy Beloved ? ' He replied : ' By comprehending and loving with all my power the beauties and the perfections of my Beloved.'

210 They asked the Lover if his Beloved had need of aught. ' Yea,' he answered, ' of those who will love and praise Him, and extol His surpassing worth.'

211　The Beloved chastened His Lover's heart with rods of love, to make him love the tree whence He plucks the rods wherewith He chastens His lovers. And this is that tree on which He suffered grief, dishonour and death, that He might bring back to love of Him those lovers whom He had lost.

212　The Lover met his Beloved, who appeared in power and glory, as One worthy of all honour. And he cried : ' How strange a thing it is that so few among men revere and know and love Thee as Thou deservest ! '　And the Beloved answered him and said : ' Greatly has man grieved Me ; for I created him to revere Me, know Me and love Me, and now, of every thousand, but a hundred fear and love Me ; and ninety of these hundred fear Me by reason of the pains of hell, and ten love Me for the sake of the glory hereafter ; hardly is there one who loves Me for My goodness and nobility.' When the Lover heard these words, he wept bitterly for the dishonour paid to his Beloved ; and he said : ' Ah, my Beloved, how much hast Thou given to man and how greatly hast Thou honoured him ! Why then has man thus forgotten Thee ? '

213　The Lover was praising his Beloved, and he said that He was transcendent because He is in a place where place is not. And therefore, when they asked the Lover where his Beloved was, he replied :

' He is, but I know not where; I only know that my Beloved is in my remembrance.'

214   The Beloved bought a slave that He might show him His graces, and made him to suffer griefs and heavy thoughts, sighs and tears.   And He asked him : ' What wilt thou eat and drink ? '   The slave replied : ' What Thou wilt.'   ' But what wilt thou ? '   ' My will is as Thine.'   ' Hast thou then no will ? ' asked the Beloved.   He answered : ' A subject and a slave has no other will than to obey his Lord and his Beloved.'

215   The Beloved inquired of His Lover if he had patience.   He answered : ' All things please me, and therefore I cannot but be patient, for he who is no more lord of his will can not be impatient.'

216   Love gave himself to any who would receive him ; and since he gave himself to few and inspired few with love, as he was free and had not been constrained, therefore the Lover cried out on Love, and accused him before the Beloved.   But Love made his defence and said : ' I strive not against free will, for I desire all lovers to have the greatest merit and glory.'

217   There was great strife and contention between Love and the Lover, because the Lover was incensed at the trials which Love made him to bear.   And

they debated whether Love or the Lover was to blame. So both of them came to the judgment-seat of the Beloved; and He chastened the Lover with griefs and rewarded him with increase of love.

218 There was a contention whether Love has more of thought than of patience. And the Lover resolved the contention, saying that Love is born of thought and nourished with patience.

219 The Lover has for neighbours the perfections of the Beloved; and the Beloved's neighbours are the thoughts of the Lover, and the trials and tears which Love gives him to bear.

220 The Lover's will loved to soar on high, that he might have great love toward his Beloved; so he commanded the understanding to soar as high as it might; and the understanding commanded the memory, so that all three mounted to the contemplation of the Beloved's glories.

221 The will of the Lover left him and flew to the Beloved. And the Beloved gave it into the captivity of the Lover, that he might use it to love and serve Him.

222 The Lover said: ' O let not my Beloved think that I have left Him to love another, for my love has united me to One, and to One alone.' The Beloved

answered and said: 'Let not My Lover think that I am loved and served by him alone; for I have many lovers who have loved Me more fervently and for longer than he.'

223 Said the Lover to his Beloved: 'O my Beloved, that art worthy of all love, Thou hast taught and accustomed my eyes to see and my ears to hear Thy wonders. And these have inspired thoughts which have brought tears to my eyes and griefs to my heart.' The Beloved answered the Lover: 'Had I not taught and guided thee so, thy name had not been written in the book of those who shall come to eternal bliss, from which are wiped out the names of such as shall go to eternal punishment.'

224 In the heart of the Lover gathered the glories and beauties of the Beloved, increasing his thoughts and griefs, so that he had altogether died if the Beloved had increased in him any further the thoughts of His greatness.

225 The Beloved came to sojourn in the hostelry of the Lover; and His Lover made Him a bed of thoughts, and there served Him sighs and tears; and the Beloved paid His reckoning with memories.

226 Love put joys and trials together into the Lover's thoughts, and the joys made complaint of

that company and accused Love before the Beloved. But when He had parted them from the sorrows which Love gives to his lovers, behold, they vanished and were gone.

227 The marks of the love which the Lover has to his Beloved are, in the beginning, tears ; then, tribulations ; and, in the end, death. And with those marks did the Lover preach before the lovers of his Beloved.

228 The Lover went into solitude ; and his heart was accompanied by thoughts, his eyes by tears, and his body by fasts and afflictions. But when the Lover returned to the companionship of men, these things went no longer with him, and the Lover remained quite alone in the company of many people.

229 Love is an ocean, its waves troubled by the winds ; it has no port or shore. The Lover perished in this ocean, and with him perished his trials, and the work of his fulfilment began.

230 ' Say, O Fool, what is love ? ' ' He answered : ' Love is a working together of thought and action towards one end, to which in like manner the Lover's will also moves ; and this is the end, that men may serve and honour his Beloved.' Think you now that the Lover's will is in truer harmony

with this end when he longs to be with his Beloved, or when he longs to convert to Him many lovers?

231 They asked the Lover: 'Who is thy Beloved?' He answered: 'He who makes me to love, desire, pine, weep, sigh and suffer, and die.'

232 They asked the Beloved: 'Who is Thy Lover?' He answered: 'He who fears naught so that he may honour and praise My Name, and who renounces all things to obey My commandments and counsels.'

233 'Say, O Fool, which is the heavier and more grievous burden—the trials of love, or the trials of those that love not?' And he answered: 'Go, ask it of those who do penance for the love of their Beloved, and of those who do penance from fear of the pains of hell.'

234 The Lover slept, and Love died, for he had naught whereby to live. The Lover wakened, and Love revived in the thoughts which the Lover sent to his Beloved.

235 The Lover said: 'The infused science comes from the will, from prayer and devotion; and acquired science comes from study and understanding.' Which of the two, then, think you, is

more proper and more pleasing to the Lover, and which possesses he the more perfectly?

236 'Say, O Fool, whence hast thou thy needs?' He answered: 'From thoughts, from longing, from adoration, from trials and from perseverance.' 'And whence hast thou all these things?' He answered: 'From love.' 'And whence hast thou thy Beloved?' 'From Himself alone.'

237 'Say, O Fool, wilt thou be free of all things?' He answered: 'Yea, save only of my Beloved.' 'Wilt thou be a prisoner?' 'Yea, of sighs and tears, thoughts and trials, dangers and exiles, that I may serve my Beloved, for to praise His exceeding worthiness was I created.'

238 Love tormented the Lover, for which cause he lamented and wept. His Beloved called him to come to Him, and be healed; and the nearer came the Lover to his Beloved, the more grievously did love afflict him; and the more he felt of love and grief, the more he loved, and the more perfectly did the Beloved heal him of his sickness.

239 Love fell sick, and the Lover tended him with patience, perseverance, obedience and hope. Love grew well, and the Lover fell sick; and he was cured by his Beloved, who made him to remember His virtue and honour.

240 'Say, O Fool, what is solitude?' He answered: 'It is solace and companionship between Lover and Beloved.' 'And what are solace and companionship?' 'Solitude in the Lover's heart, when he remembers naught save his Beloved.'

241 They asked the Lover: 'In which is there greater danger, in bearing trials for love's sake or in enjoying pleasures?' The Lover took counsel with his Beloved, and replied: 'The perils which come through pleasures are the perils of ignorance; and those which come through afflictions are the perils of impatience.'

242 The Beloved gave Love his freedom, and allowed men to take him to themselves as much as they would; but scarce one was found who would take him to his heart. And for this cause the Lover wept, and was sad at the dishonour which is paid to Love by the ungrateful among men and by false lovers.

243 Love destroyed all that was in the heart of his faithful Lover that he might live and have free course in it; and the Lover would have died had memory not revealed to him his Beloved.

244 On two things the Lover was wont to meditate: the one was the Essence and the goodness of

his Beloved, and the other was his Beloved's works. He knew not which of these was the more excellent and the more pleasing to the Beloved.

245 'Say, O Fool, wouldst thou fain die?' He answered: 'Yea, to the pleasures of this world and the thoughts of the unhappy sinners who dishonour and forget my Beloved; in whose thoughts I would have no part nor lot, since my Beloved has no part in them.'

246 'If thou speakest truth, O Fool, thou wilt be beaten by men, tormented, mocked, reproved and killed.' He answered: 'From those words it follows that if I spoke falsehoods I should be praised by men, served, loved and honoured, and defended by those who despise my Beloved.'

247 False flatterers were speaking ill of the Lover one day in the presence of his Beloved. The Lover was patient, and the Beloved shewed His justice, wisdom and power. And the Lover preferred to be blamed and reproved in this wise, than to be one of those that falsely accused him.

248 The Beloved planted many seeds in the heart of His Lover, but one of them only took life and put forth leaf and gave flower and fruit. Think you that from this single fruit may come many seeds?

249   Far above Love is the Beloved ; far beneath it
is the Lover ; and Love, which lies between these
two, made the Beloved to descend to the Lover,
and the Lover to rise toward the Beloved.   And this
ascending and descending is the being and the life
of Love—of that Love which makes the Lover to
endure pain and which ever serves the Beloved.

250   On the right side of Love stands the Beloved,
and on the left side is the Lover ; and thus he
cannot reach the Beloved unless he pass through
Love.   And before Love stands the Beloved, and
beyond is the Lover ; so that the Lover cannot
reach Love unless his thoughts and desires have
first passed through the Beloved.

251   The Beloved clothed Himself in the garment
of His Lover, that he might be His companion in
glory for ever.   So the Lover desired to wear
crimson garments daily, that his dress might be like
that of his Beloved.

252   ' Say, O Fool, what did thy Beloved before the
world was ? '   He answered : ' My Beloved loved,
because of His manifold properties, eternal, personal,
and infinite, in which are Lover, Love and Beloved.'

253   The Lover wept and was sad, when he saw
how the unbelievers were losing his Beloved
through ignorance ; but he rejoiced in the justice

of his Beloved, who punishes those that know Him and are disobedient. Which, think you, was greater, his sorrow or his joy? And was his joy greater when he saw his Beloved honoured than his sorrow at seeing Him despised?

254 The Lover contemplated his Beloved in all the variety and harmony of His virtues; and again in the contrariety between virtue and vice; and again in His Being and perfection, which have greater harmony between themselves than non-existence and imperfection.

255 The variety and harmony which the Lover found in the Beloved revealed to him His secrets, to wit, His plurality and unity, to the greater concordance of essence without contrariety.

256 They said to the Lover: ' Corruption is contrary to being, as generation, which is opposed to it, is the contrary of non-existence. If it were eternally corrupting and corrupted, it would be impossible that non-existence or end should harmonise with corruption.' By these words the Lover saw in his Beloved the principle of eternal generation.

257 If that which increases the love of the Lover for his Beloved were falseness, that which diminished it would be truth. And if this were so, it would follow that there would be a want of the

great and the true in the Beloved, and that there would be harmony in Him between the false and the mean.

258 The Lover praised his Beloved, and said that if in Him were the greatest degree of perfection and the greatest possible freedom from imperfection, his Beloved must be simple, pure and present in essence and operation. And while the Lover praised his Beloved thus, there was revealed to him the Trinity of his Beloved.

259 In the numbers 1 and 3 the Lover found greater harmony than between any others, because by these numbers every bodily form passed to existence from non-existence. And the greatest harmony of number, the Lover thought, was in the Unity and the Trinity of his Beloved.

260 The Lover extolled the power, the wisdom and the will of his Beloved, who had created all things, save only sin ; so that, but for His power and wisdom and will, had nothing existed. And neither the power, the wisdom nor the will of the Beloved are an occasion of sin.

261 The Lover praised and loved his Beloved, for He had created him and given him all things ; and he praised and loved Him too because it pleased Him to take his form and nature. And it may be

asked, Which had more of perfection, his praise or his love?

262   Love tempted the wisdom of the Lover, and asked him whether the Beloved showed the greater love in taking his nature, or in redeeming him. And the Lover was perplexed, and replied at last that redemption was destined to put away un-happiness, and the Incarnation to bring about bliss.   And this reply provoked the question again : ' Which was the greater love ? '

263   The Lover went from door to door asking alms to keep in mind the love of his Beloved for His servants, and to practise the virtues of poverty, humility and patience, which are well-pleasing to the Beloved.

264   They asked pardon of the Lover, for the love of his Beloved ; and the Lover not only pardoned them but gave them himself and his goods.

265   With tears in his eyes the Lover described the Passion and the pains which his Beloved bore for love of him ; and with sad and heavy thoughts he wrote down the words which He uttered ; and by mercy and hope he was comforted.

266   The Beloved taught His Lover how to love ; and Love instructed him in speech ; and Patience,

to bear afflictions for the love of Him to whom he had given himself to be a servant.

267 The Beloved asked men if they had seen His Lover, and they asked Him: 'What are the qualities of Thy Lover?' And the Beloved said: 'My Lover is ardent yet fearful; rich and yet poor; joyful, sad and pensive; and every day he grieves because of his love.'

268 They asked the Lover: 'Wilt thou sell thy desire?' He answered: 'I have sold it already to my Beloved, for such a price as would buy the whole world.'

269 'Preach, O Fool, speak concerning thy Beloved; weep and fast.' So the Lover renounced the world, and went forth lovingly to seek his Beloved, and to praise Him in those places wherein He was dishonoured.

270 The Lover builded a fair city wherein his Beloved might dwell; of love, thoughts, tears, complaints and griefs he builded it; with joy, devotion and hope he adorned it; and with justice, prudence, faith, fortitude and temperance he furnished it.

271 The Lover drank of love at the fountain of the Beloved, and there the Beloved washed the

Lover's feet, though many a time he had despised and forgotten His greatness, and the world had suffered thereby.

272 ' Say, O Fool, what is sin ? ' He answered : ' It is the turning and directing of the intention away from the final Cause and Intention for which all things have been created by my Beloved.'

273 The Lover saw that the world was created so that eternity should be more in harmony with his Beloved, who is Infinite Essence of greatness and all perfection, than with the world, which is a finite quantity ; and therefore the justice of his Beloved was before time and finite quantities were.

274 The Lover defended his Beloved against those who said that the world is eternal, saying that the justice of his Beloved would not be perfect, if He restored not to every man his own body, and for this no place or material order would suffice ; nor, if the world were eternal, could it be ordered for one end only ; and yet, if it were not so ordered, there would be wanting in his Beloved perfection of wisdom and will.

275 ' Say, O Fool, wherein is the beginning of wisdom ? ' He answered : ' In faith and devotion, which are a ladder whereby understanding may rise to a comprehension of the secrets of my Beloved.'

276 ' Where then have faith and devotion their beginning ? ' He answered : ' In my Beloved, who illumines faith and nurtures devotion.'

277 They asked the Lover : ' Which is greater—the possible or the impossible ? ' He answered : ' The possible is greater in man, and the impossible in my Beloved, since power and possibility are in agreement, and impossibility and actuality.'

278 ' Say, O Fool, which is the greater—difference or harmony ? ' He answered : ' Save in my Beloved, difference is greater in plurality, and harmony in unity ; but in my Beloved they are equal in plurality and in unity.'

279 ' Say, O Lover, what is true worth ? ' He answered : ' It is the opposite of this world's worth, which false and vainglorious lovers desire ; for they go after worth and achieve only worthlessness.'

280 ' Say, O Fool, hast thou seen one without his reason ? ' He answered : ' I have seen a lord of the Church, who had many cups on his table, and many plates and knives of silver, and in his chamber had many garments and a great bed, and in his coffers great wealth—and at the gates of his palace but few poor.'

281 ' Knowest thou, O Fool, what is evil ? ' He answered : ' Evil thoughts.' ' And what is

loyalty ? ' ' It is fear of my Beloved, born of charity and of shame which men reproach.' ' And what is honour ? ' He answered : ' It is to think on my Beloved, to desire Him and to praise His glorious Name.'

282   The Lover went one day into a cloister, and the monks inquired of him if he, too, were a religious. ' Yea,' he answered, ' of the order of my Beloved.' ' What rule dost thou follow ? ' He answered : ' My Beloved's.' ' To whom art thou vowed ? ' He said : ' To my Beloved.' ' Hast thou thy will ? ' He answered : ' Nay, it is given to my Beloved.' ' Hast thou added aught to the rule of thy Beloved ? ' He answered : ' Naught can be added to that which is already perfect. And why,' continued the Lover, ' do not you that are religious take the Name of my Beloved ?   May it not be that, as you bear the name of another, your love may grow less, and, hearing the voice of another, you may not catch the voice of the Beloved ? '

283   The trials and tribulations that the Lover endured for love's sake made him weary and apt to be impatient ; and the Beloved reproved him, saying that he whom either trouble or happiness affected thus knew but little of love.   So the Lover was contrite and wept, and he begged his Beloved to restore his love again.

284 ' Say, O Fool, what is love ? ' He answered :
' Love is that which throws the free into bondage,
and to those that are in bonds gives liberty.' And
who can say whether in love there is more of liberty
or of bondage ?

285 The Beloved called His Lover, and he
answered Him, saying : ' What wilt Thou, O my
Beloved, Thou who art the sight of my eyes, thought
of my thoughts, love of my love and sum of my perfections,—yea, and the source of all my beginnings ? '

286 ' O my Beloved,' said the Lover, ' I come to
Thee, I walk in Thee, for Thou dost call me.
And I greet Thee with Thine own Sign, by which
I hope for eternal life and eternal blessing.'

287 The Lover cried aloud and said : ' Fire gives
warmth, its heat gives lightness, and that lightness
draws on high. And in like manner love inflames
the thoughts, gives lightness and draws on high.
And one love unites three things, binding them
securely the one to the others.'

288 They asked the Lover : ' What is the world ? '
He answered : ' It is a book for such as can read, in
which is revealed my Beloved.' They asked him :
' Is thy Beloved, then, in the world ? ' He answered :
' Yea, even as the writer is in his book.' ' And
wherein consists this book ? ' He answered : ' In

my Beloved, since my Beloved contains it all, and therefore is the world in my Beloved rather than my Beloved in the world.'

289 ' Say, O Lover, who is he that loves and seems to thee as a fool ? ' The Lover answered : ' He that loves the shadow and makes no account of the truth.' ' And whom dost thou call rich ? ' ' He that loves truth.' ' And who is poor ? ' ' He that loves falsehood.'

290 They asked the Lover : ' Is the world to be loved ? ' He answered : ' Truly it is, but as a piece of work, for its artificer's sake, or as the night by reason of the day which follows it.'

291 The Lover cried out to his Lord concerning his Beloved, and to his Beloved concerning his Lord. And the Lord and the Beloved said : ' Who is this that makes division in Us, that are One only ? ' The Lover answered and said : ' It is pity, which belongs to the Lord, and tribulation, which comes through the Beloved.'

292 The Lover was in peril in the great ocean of love, and he trusted in his Beloved, who came to him with troubles, thoughts, tears, sighs and griefs ; for the ocean was of love.

293 The Lover rejoiced in the Being of his Be-

loved, for (said he) from His Being is all other Being derived, and by It sustained, and made subject and constrained to honour and serve my Beloved. By no being can He be condemned or destroyed, or made greater or less.

294 'What is the Being of thy Beloved?' He answered: 'It is a bright ray throughout all things, even as the sun which shines over all the world. For if it withdraw its brightness, it leaves all things in darkness, and when it shines forth it brings the day. Even more so is my Beloved.'

295 My Beloved is one, and in His unity my thoughts and my love are united in one will; my Beloved's unity is the source of all unities and all pluralities; and His plurality of all pluralities and unities.

296 'O Beloved, by Thy greatness my desires, my thoughts and my afflictions are made great; for so great art Thou that all things which have remembrance and joy and understanding of Thee are great; and Thy greatness makes all things small which are contrary to Thy honour and commandments.'

297 'Thou knowest my sinfulness, O Beloved; be merciful, then, and pardon. Thou knowest better than I who Thou art; yet even I know Thy pardon and love, since Thou hast awakened in me

contrition and pain, and the desire to die a shameful death that Thy Name may be thereby exalted.'

298   ' Thy power, O Beloved, can save me through Thy goodness, mercy and pardon, yet it can condemn me through Thy justice, and my failures and imperfections. But let Thy power work its will in me, for it is wholly perfection, whether it bring salvation or eternal punishment.'

299   ' O Truth that I love, visit my contrite heart, draw water from mine eyes, that my will may love Thee ; and since Thy truth, O Beloved, is sovereign, draw truth from my will, that I may honour Thy Name, and cause it to hate my shortcomings.'

300   The Lover gazed at the rainbow, and it seemed to him as though it were of three colours. And he cried : ' O marvellous distinction of three, for the three together are one ! And how can this be in the image, unless it be so of itself, in truth ? '

301   The Beloved created, and the Lover destroyed. The Beloved judged, and the Lover wept. Then the Beloved created glory again for the Lover. The Beloved finished His work, and the Lover remained for ever in the companionship of his Beloved.

302   By verdant paths, with feeling, imagination, understanding and will, the Lover went in search of

his Beloved. And in those paths the Lover endured griefs and perils for his Beloved's sake, that he might lift up his will and understanding to his Beloved, who wills that His lovers may comprehend and love Him exceedingly.

303 The perfection of the Beloved uplifted His Lover, and his own shortcomings cast him down. Which of these two forces, think you, has by nature the greater power over the Lover?

304 'Thou hast placed me, O my Beloved, between my evil and Thy good. On Thy part may there be mercy and pity, patience, humility, pardon, restoration and help; on mine let there be contrition, perseverance and remembrance of Thy sacred Passion, with sighs and tears.'

305 'O Beloved, that makest me to love, if Thou aidest me not, why didst Thou will to create me, and why didst Thou endure grief for my sake and bear Thy so grievous Passion? Since Thou didst help me thus to rise, my Beloved, help me also to descend to the remembrance and hatred of my faults and failings, that my thoughts may the better rise again to desire, honour and praise Thee.'

306 'My will, O Beloved, hast Thou made free to love Thy honour or despise Thy worth, that in my will my love to Thee may be increased; and in

granting me this liberty, O Beloved, hast Thou put my will into danger. Remember, then, Thy Lover in this danger, that I may place in servitude my free will, praise Thy honour, and multiply tears and grief in my heart.'

307 ' O Beloved, never from Thee came fault nor failing to Thy Lover, nor can Thy Lover attain to perfection but through Thy grace and mercy. Then, since the Lover has Thee in such possessions, do Thou remember him in his perils and tribulations.'

308 ' O Beloved, who in one Name, Jesus Christ, art called both God and Man, by that Name my will seeks to adore Thee as God and Man. And if Thou, Beloved, hast so greatly honoured Thy Lover, through none of his merits, why honourest Thou not so many ignorant men, who knowingly have been less guilty of dishonouring Thy Name, Jesus Christ, than has this Thy Lover ? '

309 The Lover wept, and he spake to his Beloved in these words : ' O Beloved, never wert Thou sparing or aught but liberal to Thy Lover, in giving him being or in granting him many creatures to serve him. Then wherefore, O Beloved, Thou who art sovereign liberality, shouldst Thou be slow to give Thy Lover tears, thoughts, griefs, wisdom and

love that he may do honour to Thy Name? So then, O Beloved, Thy Lover asks of Thee long life that he may receive of Thee many of the gifts aforesaid.'

310 'O Beloved, if Thou dost help just men against their mortal enemies, help to increase my thoughts and desires for Thy honour. And if Thou dost help sinners to lead just lives, help Thy Lover that he may sacrifice his will to Thy glory; and as to his body, that he may tread the martyr's path as a testimony of love.'

311 The Lover made complaint to his Beloved of temptations which came to him daily to disturb his thoughts. And the Beloved answered him: 'Such temptations are occasions of recourse to the memory, that the lover may think upon God and love His grace and honour.'

312 The Beloved had mercy upon His Lover, because of His perfect love, and because of His Lover's needs. Which of those two reasons, think you, moved the Beloved the more strongly to forgive His Lover's sins?

313 Our Lady and the Saints and angels in glory cried to my Beloved: 'Remember the errors into which the world has fallen through ignorance, but

remember how great is Thy justice, O Beloved, and how great the ignorance of Thine enemies.'

314   The Lover lifted up the powers of his soul, and mounted the ladder of humanity to glory in the Divine Nature ; and from the Divine Nature the powers of his soul descended, to glory in the human nature of his Beloved.

315   The straiter are the paths along which the Lover journeys to his Beloved, the vaster is his love ; and the straiter his love, the broader are the paths. So that however it be the Lover receives love, trials and griefs, comforts and joys from his Beloved.

316   Love comes from love, thoughts from thoughts and tears from griefs ; and love leads to love, as thoughts lead to tears and griefs to sighs.   And the Beloved watches His Lover, who bears all these afflictions for His love.

317   The desires of the Lover and his memories of the Beloved's greatness kept vigils and went on journeys and pilgrimages.   And they brought to the Lover graces which lit up his understanding and made his will to increase in love.

318   With his imagination the Lover formed and pictured his Beloved's Countenance in bodily wise, and with his understanding he beautified It in

spiritual things ; and with his will he worshipped It in all creatures.

319 The Lover purchased a day of tears with another of thoughts ; and a day of love came through a day of tribulations ; and both his thoughts and his love were increased.

320 The Lover was in a far country, and he forgot his Beloved, but was sad at the absence of his lord, his wife, his children and his friends. But soon the memory of his Beloved returned to him, that he might be comforted, and that his exile might cause him neither vexation nor sorrow.

321 The Lover heard his Beloved's words ; his understanding beheld Him in them ; his will had pleasure in that which he heard ; and his memory recalled his Beloved's virtues and His promises.

322 The Lover heard men speak evil of his Beloved, and in this evil-speaking his understanding perceived his Beloved's justice and patience ; for His justice would punish the evil-speakers, while His patience would await their contrition and repentance. In which of these two think you that the Lover believed more earnestly ?

323 The Lover fell sick, and made his testament with the counsel of his Beloved. His sins and

faults he bequeathed to penance and contrition; worldly pleasures to contempt. To his eyes he left tears; to his heart sighs of love; to his understanding his Beloved's graces, and to his memory the Passion which his Beloved endured for love of him. And to his activity he bequeathed the guidance of unbelievers, who go to their doom through ignorance.

324 The scent of flowers brought to the Lover's mind the evil stench of riches and meanness, of old age and lasciviousness, of discontent and pride. The taste of sweet things recalled to him the bitterness of temporal possessions and of entering and quitting this world. The enjoyment of earthly pleasures made him feel how quickly this world passes, and how the delights which are here so pleasant may be the occasion of eternal torments.

325 The Lover endured hunger and thirst, cold and heat, poverty and nakedness, sickness and tribulations; and he would have died had he not had remembrance of his Beloved, who healed him with hope and memory, with the renunciation of this world and contempt for the revilings of men.

326 The Lover made his bed between trials and joys : in joys he lay down to sleep and in trials he awakened. Which of these two, think you, was nearer to the bed of the Lover ?

327 In anger the Lover lay down to sleep, resenting the revilings of men; in patience he awakened, remembering his Beloved. Which, think you, did the Lover feel the more deeply—the love of his Beloved or the scorn of men?

328 The Lover thought upon death, and he was afraid, until he remembered the city of his Beloved, to which love and death are the gates and the entrance.

329 Two men were disputing concerning simplicity, the one against the other. And the one said : ' The simple man is he who knows nothing.' The other said : ' The simple man is he who lives without sin.' And the Lover came and said : ' True simplicity has he who commits all his ways to my Beloved.'

330 ' For simplicity is to exalt faith above understanding, which it so far exceeds, and in all that pertains to my Beloved it is to avoid completely all things vain, superfluous, curious, over-subtle and presumptuous. For all these are contrary to simplicity.'

331 Another time they both inquired of him, asking that he would tell them if the science of the simple is a great one. He answered : ' The science of great sages is as a great heap of a few grains, but

the science of the simple is a small heap of number-
less grains, because neither presumption nor
curiosity nor over-subtlety are added to the heap
of simple men.' ' And what is the work of presumption and curiosity ? ' The Lover replied :
' Vanity is the mother of curiosity, and pride is the
mother of presumption, and therefore is their work
the work of vanity and pride. And the enemies of
my Beloved are known by presumption and curiosity,
even as love for Him is acquired by simplicity.'

332 The Lover lost a jewel which he greatly
prized, and was sorely distressed, until his Beloved
put to him this question : ' Which profiteth thee
more, the jewel that thou hadst or thy patience in all
the acts of thy Beloved ? '

333 Many lovers came together, and they asked
Love's messenger where and in what thing the
heart was most ardently inflamed with devotion
and love. Love's messenger answered : ' In the
House of God, when we humble ourselves and
adore Him with all our powers ; for He alone is
Holiest of the holy. And those that know not
how to do this, know not what it is truly to love
Him.'

334 The Lover thought upon his sins, and for fear
of hell he would fain have wept, but he could not.

So he begged Love to give him tears, and Wisdom answered that he muſt weep earneſtly and often, but for the love of his Beloved rather than for the pains of hell; for tears of love are more pleasing to Him than tears shed through fear.

335   The Lover obeyed Wisdom; and, on the one hand, he shed many and great tears for love's sake, and, on the other, few and small tears for fear, that by love and not by fear he might honour his Beloved. And the tears which he shed for love brought him solace and reſt, while the tears of fear gave him sorrow and tribulation.

336   The Lover fell asleep while thinking on the trials and the obſtacles which he met in serving his Beloved; and he feared leſt through those hindrances his works might be loſt.   But the Beloved sent consciousness to him, and he awakened to the merits and powers of his Beloved.

337   The Lover had to journey long over roads that were rough and hard; and the time came when he should set out, carrying the heavy burden that Love makes his lovers to bear.   So the Lover unburdened his soul of the cares and pleasures of this world, that his heart might bear the weight with more ease, and his soul journey along those roads in its Beloved's company.

338 Before the Lover, one day, they spoke ill of the Beloved, and the Lover made neither reply nor defence of his Beloved. Which, think you, was the more to be blamed, the men who spoke ill of the Beloved, or the Lover who was silent and defended Him not?

339 As the Lover contemplated his Beloved, his understanding conceived subtleties and his will loved Him more and more. In which of the two think you that memory grew more fruitful in thinking on the Beloved?

340 With fervour and fear the Lover journeyed abroad to honour his Beloved. Fervour bore him along and fear preserved him from danger. And while the Lover was journeying thus, he found sighs and tears, which brought him greetings from his Beloved. Through which of these four companions think you that the Lover received the greatest consolation in his Beloved?

341 The Lover gazed upon himself that he might be a mirror in which to behold his Beloved; and he gazed upon his Beloved, as in a mirror wherein he could learn to know himself. Which of these two mirrors, think you, was the nearer to his understanding?

342 They asked the Lover in what manner the

heart of man was turned towards the love of his
Beloved. He answered them and said : ' Even as
the sunflower turns to the sun.' ' How is it, then,
that all men love not thy Beloved ? ' He answered :
' They that love Him not have night in their hearts,
because of their sin.'

343 Theology and Philosophy, Medicine and Law
met the Lover, who asked them if they had seen his
Beloved. The first wept, the second was doubtful,
but the other two were glad. What, think you,
was the meaning of these happenings to the Lover
that was seeking his Beloved ?

344 Full of tears and anguish the Lover went in
search of his Beloved, by the path of the senses and
also by the intellectual road. Which of those two
ways, think you, did he enter first, as he went after
his Beloved ? And in which of them did the
Beloved reveal Himself to him the more openly ?

345 The Lover met an astrologer, and inquired
of him : ' What means thy astrology ? ' He replied : ' It is a science that foretells things to come.'
' Thou art deceived,' said the Lover ; ' it is no
science, but one falsely so called. It is necromancy,
or the black art, in disguise, and the science of
deceiving and lying prophets which dishonour the
work of the sovereign Master. At all times it has

been the messenger of evil tidings; and it runs clean contrary to the providence of my Beloved, for in place of the evils which it threatens He promises good things.'

346 The Lover went forth, crying: 'Oh, how vain are all they who follow after lust of knowledge and presumption! For through lust of knowledge do they fall into the greatest depths of impiety, insulting the Name of God and with curses and incantations invoking evil spirits as good angels, investing them with the names of God and of good angels, and profaning holy things with figures and images and by writings. And through presumption all errors are implanted in the world.' And the Lover wept bitterly, for all the insults which are offered to his Beloved by ignorant men.

347 At the Day of Judgment the Beloved will cause all that men have given Him in this world to be placed on one side, and on the other side all that they have given to the world. Thus it shall be clearly seen to what extent they have loved Him, and which of their two gifts is the greater and nobler.

348 The Lover's will was enamoured of itself and the understanding asked: 'Is it more like the Beloved to love oneself or to love the Beloved? For the Beloved is to be loved more than anything

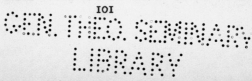

beside.' With what answer, think you, could the will make reply to the understanding most truly?

349 'Say, O Fool, what is the greatest and noblest love to be found in the creature?' He answered: 'That which is one with the Creator.' 'And why so?' 'Because there is nothing with which the Creator can make nobler a creature.'

350 One day the Lover was at prayer, and he perceived that he wept not; and in order that he might weep he bade his thoughts to think upon wealth, and women, and sons, and meats, and vainglory. And his understanding found that more men have each of the things aforesaid to their servants than has his Beloved. And thereupon were his eyes wet with tears, and his soul was in sorrow and pain.

351 One day the Lover was looking towards the east, and towards the west, towards the south and towards the north, and he espied the Sign of his Beloved. And therefore he caused that Sign to be engraven, and at each of its four extremities he had a precious jewel set, as bright as the sun. That Sign he wore ever upon him, and it brought the Truth to his remembrance.

352 The Lover was walking pensively, thinking on his Beloved, and he found on the way many people

and great multitudes who asked him for news. And the Lover, who was rejoicing in his Beloved, gave them not that which they asked of him, and said that he could not reply to their words without departing far from his Beloved.

353 Behind and before was the Lover vested in love, and he went seeking his Beloved. Love said to him : 'Where goest thou, O Lover ? ' He answered : ' I go to my Beloved, that thou mayest be increased.'

354 ' Say, O Fool, what is Religion ? ' He answered : ' Purity of thought, and longing for death by which the Beloved may be honoured, and renouncing the world, that nothing may hinder one from contemplating Him and speaking truth of His Name.'

355 ' Say, O Fool, what are trials, sighs, laments, afflictions, perils, tears ? ' He answered : ' The joys of the Beloved.' ' And why are they so ? ' ' That He may be the more deeply loved by reason of them, and the Lover be the more bounteously rewarded.'

356 The Lover passed through divers places and found many men who were rejoicing, laughing and singing and living in great joy and comfort. And he wondered if this world were meant for laughing or for weeping.

357   So the Virtues came, to pronounce upon that question. And Faith said : ' It is for weeping, because the faithless are more in number than the believers.'   Hope said : ' It is for weeping, because few are those that hope in God, whereas many put their trust in the riches of earth.'   Charity said : ' It is for weeping, because so few are those that love God and their neighbour.'   And there followed the other Virtues, and so declared they all.

358   The lovers sought to prove Love's messenger, and they said that they should go through the world, crying that worshippers must honour servants as servants and the Lord as a lord, so that their requests might better be heard, and because there needs not to love, save the Beloved.

359   They asked Love's messenger whence came to the Beloved so many useless servants, viler, more abject, and more contemptible than secular men. Love's messenger answered and said : ' They come through the fault of those whose task it is to furnish their Sovereign,—the King of Kings,—the Beloved,—with servants.   They make no question, as they ought, concerning the wisdom nor the lives nor the habits of those whom they choose.   And those whom they will not take for His train they allow to serve the Eternal King in His palace, and in the most holy ministry of His Table.   Wherefore

ought they to fear the severest retributions when they are called by the Beloved to their account.'

360 They asked the Lover : ' In which is love greater, in the Lover who lives or in the Lover who dies ? ' He answered : ' In the Lover who dies.' ' And why ? ' ' Because in one who lives for love it may yet be greater, but in one who dies for love it can be no greater.'

361 Two lovers met : the one revealed his Beloved, and the other learned of Him. And it was disputed which of those two was nearer to his Beloved ; and in the solution the Lover took knowledge of the demonstration of the Trinity.

362 ' Say, O Fool, why dost thou speak with such subtlety ? ' He answered : ' That I may raise my understanding to the height of my Beloved's greatness, and that thereby more men may honour, love and serve Him.'

363 The Lover drank deeply of the wine of memory, understanding and love for his Beloved. And that wine the Beloved made bitter with His Lover's tears.

364 Love heated and inflamed the Lover with remembrance of his Beloved ; and the Beloved cooled his ardour, with sorrows and tears and forgetfulness of the delights of this world, and the

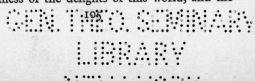

renunciation of vainglories. So his love grew, when he remembered wherefore he suffered grief and affliction, and the men of the world persecutions and trials.

365   They asked the Lover this question: 'Wherein dies love?' The Lover answered: 'In the delights of this world.' 'And whence has it life and sustenance?' 'In thoughts of the world to come.' Wherefore they that had inquired of him prepared to renounce this world, that they might think the more deeply upon the next, and that their love might live and find nourishment.

366   'Say, O Fool, what is this world?' He answered: 'It is the prison-house of those that love and serve my Beloved.' 'And who is he that imprisons them?' He answered: 'Conscience, love, fear, renunciation and contrition, and the companionship of wilful men.' 'And who is he that frees them?' 'Mercy, pity and justice.' 'And where are they then sent?' 'To eternal bliss, and the joyful company of true lovers, where they shall laud, bless and glorify the Beloved everlastingly, to whom be ever given praise, honour and glory throughout all the world.'

Printed in England at THE BALLANTYNE PRESS
SPOTTISWOODE, BALLANTYNE & CO. LTD.
Colchester, London & Eton

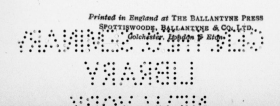